air lock

A sacred space to meet with God

Becoming

Themes: Sadness, Depression

Tears for fears

Decompress
The most I think I ever cried
Was when my girlfriend left;
For weeks and weeks I could have died.
I felt totally bereft.
A lot of tears I must have shed
But not enough to wet the bed.

NOW READ PSALM 6

Immerse
When did you last cry and why? I blubbed the other week when my girlfriend left for university, because I knew how much I'd miss her. Generally things that bring a tear to my eye are girl-related grief, sad films (*Ghost* used to be a particular culprit), when I get frustrated, and those telly programmes where they show African mothers being reunited with their kids who disappeared six years ago during a civil war. Some of those are superficial compared to others, and compared to stuff like bereavement. But subjectively, if something makes us cry then it must be fairly important.

>I don't think I've ever cried in the way David describes in this psalm. He's obviously having a seriously hard time. He'd been punished by God with an illness, and judging by what he says in verse 5, he doesn't reckon he's got long left. To make matters worse, his enemies are taking advantage of his condition to vent their antagonism. It puts some of our worries into perspective, doesn't it?

Re-engage
Are we this emotional and passionate in our prayers? Do we show God our raw feelings, or do we just give him the person we think he wants to see? Don't be afraid to literally CRY out to him. This psalm also challenges us to have faith in the hardest times, when it looks like all else is lost. When we feel like that, can we truly say it's him we turn to?

>Today when you pray, be honest with God about what you're feeling. Sometimes we should be crying when we pray. But likewise we should always be praying when we cry. Take time today to give hope to those who can't see past their tears.

Airlock: Becoming

Fair-ground attraction

Themes: Fairness, Unfair

Decompress
I've said it many times in prayer
'Jesus, life is so unfair.'
Others get away with stuff
While I just can't do enough.
Sometimes crime does seem to pay
But What Would Jesus Do today?

NOW READ PSALM 7

Immerse
The Tribe had an album out a few years ago called *We Don't Get What We Deserve*. However, a book I've been reading called *What's So Amazing About Grace?* (by Philip Yancey) talks about the other side of the coin, that we in fact, get what we don't deserve. In simple terms, according to the Bible, sinners deserve death. We are sinners, but because of the cross, we don't get the punishment we deserve.

>In this psalm, David is calling for God to dish out punishment to those who deserve it, including himself. 'If I've done something wrong, then let me be punished for it' is a tough call to make. But how I'd love to be able to say verse 8 and sincerely mean it. I hate guilt, knowing I've done wrong, knowing I've sinned. I wish I could utter that verse and be convinced it was true.

>'God, you do what is right' (v 9) can be read two ways. On the one hand it can be seen as an affirmation that God is perfect, that he's in control. David could be praising this aspect of God's character. He could also intend it to be taken as 'God, please do what is right, in this situation now.' David wanted God to deal with his enemies and those doing evil, and it fits with that, as well as being consistent with the other verses of praise found in the psalm.

Re-engage
Sometimes we look at friends or others who aren't Christians, and it seems that they're having a great time. They get drunk, sleep around, fiddle their tax, and get away with it all. But life for the Christian isn't about what we can get away with, it's about how close to God we can stay. Verses 14–16 show that crime and sin do not pay in the long run.

>Thank God today that you don't get what you deserve. Ask him to show you the wrong things in your life that need sorting. And pray that one day you'll be able to say, 'I have done no wrong…'

Airlock: Becoming

Themes: Importance, Creation

The human league

Decompress

Twinkle, twinkle little star
God set things the way they are.
Up above the world so high
He looks down on you and I
Though you twinkle through the night
To him you're never out of sight.

NOW READ PSALM 8

Immerse

I've recently been travelling round the world. One of the most amazing things you see when you travel in desert areas is the sky at night. I've seen sunsets and sunrises that I'll always remember, and stars and planets I may never see again because constellations are different in the southern hemisphere.

>In the outback of Australia and the plains of Africa I sat and looked and marvelled at the stars. I imagine I felt how David did when he wrote parts of this psalm. Why am I so important to God, when clearly he made much bigger and more impressive things in the universe than puny little me?

>In verse 3, David refers back to the start of Genesis, where he can relate what he sees in the night sky to the biblical account of creation. Although he then doubts the importance of man, he's able to put man into context by looking at his role on earth – lower than the heavenly beings, but at the same time given the responsibility of being God's stewards, in charge of the earth and all it contains.

>The writer to the Hebrews uses verses 4–6 to describe Jesus. Which shouldn't make us feel out of place in this world, rather that he has been here and already shown us our place, responsibilities and how to live.

Re-engage

Do you ever feel totally insignificant in comparison to more important stuff? If you do, try putting it into perspective by asking 'Would God have sent his son to die for me if I was insignificant to him?' I think not.

>This psalm shows us that as well as having the purpose on this earth of telling others the good news of Jesus, we are also to look after the world God made. Recycling, walking-not-driving, buying free-range eggs… Make a list of things today that you think you should be doing to look after God's world, from the small things (like above) to the bigger ones.

Airlock: Becoming

| Themes: | Anger, Thanksgiving |

5 star service

Decompress
Sometimes we can quickly forget
The things that God has done;
But looking back along our track
Shows he's the faithful one.

NOW READ PSALM 9

Immerse
I'm one of those people who sometimes finds it hard to let things that should be in the past stay there; do you know what I mean? It's easy to look back in anger at that person who treated you badly, or at that situation you failed in etc... But this psalm is really about looking back, not in anger, but in thanks. David's taking the time to look at all the stuff that's happened recently, and is thanking God for it.

>I know that I'm certainly very keen to pray and ask for loads of things, but a bit slower to thank God for them afterwards. I could definitely do with taking a leaf out of David's book.

>David's enemies seem to have got what they deserved. God has had mercy on David and has spared him, and God has heard the cries of his servant and answered his prayers. And now David is doing the right thing in turning round and praising God for what he has done.

Re-engage
Our response to this should be to take a look at what has been happening in our lives recently. Has God answered some of your prayers (though not necessarily with the answer you may have wanted)? Have you thanked him for his faithfulness to you? If you haven't, then it's definitely time to start thinking about it.

>I've just started writing a spiritual journal where I write down things, not every day, just now and then, that seem important to me. It might be a sermon point from church on Sunday or a verse I read in quiet time. I often write down stuff I'm worried about, and the good thing about having it all down on paper is that when you look back, you can see how things have worked out, how prayers have been answered and how God was with you all along. I highly recommend doing it... well, go on then!

Airlock: Becoming

Themes: Disasters, Where is God?

Angry anderson

Decompress

Where was God when this went wrong?
Why did we have to wait so long?
I can't believe he's staying silent
When all around, the world is violent.
When will he come and do something?
He did, he sent his Son, the King.

NOW READ PSALM 10

Immerse

The kind of things described in this psalm are pretty hard for the writer to stomach, and he asks, 'Where is God in this?' I think it's ironic that this comes straight after a psalm that basically says, 'When I look back, I can see that God was here, did this and answered that prayer.' But I guess that's the point. We shouldn't let go of what we know in times when we think God has let go of us. It's not wrong to doubt where God is, but we need to remember the things he has done for us in the past and have faith, as David has through this series of psalms, that he will reveal himself in the future, in his own time.

>Have you ever seriously doubted the existence of God because things have gone so wrong? At the time of writing this, one of my flatmates has just been dumped by his girlfriend of three years for someone else, and my other flatmate's mum recently announced she'd been having an affair for over four years and was leaving her husband after 26 years of marriage. Where is God there? When a former girlfriend cheated on me a few years ago, I asked that very question. But people said to me, 'When things like this happen to others, you'll be able to help them through.' And it's true. I'm not being big-headed when I say that in the situation with my two mates, God is there, working through people like me to help them make sense of it. It's not always a case of 'Where is God?', but more 'How is God working and through whom?'

Re-engage

If you know someone who is going through a hard time, think about how you can help them. Have you been through things that can help you relate to them? Do you know how they're feeling? Do you have advice from previous experiences that you can give them. Remember, if we believe that God has a plan for our lives, then everything happens for a reason. We can be used to help others, in the same way that others are used to help us.

Airlock: Becoming

When was the last time you cried in the presence of God?
How does coming to him with your sadness make it more bearable?
Looking back, think about times when your faith has remained strong despite your circumstances.

Extra_1 Isaiah 61:1-11
Extra_2 Revelation 7:9-17

Themes: Unity, Denominations

No logo

Decompress

What kind of a Christian are you? A Soul-Survivor-ite, a Greenbelter, a Spring Harvest groupie or an 'all festivals are boring' stay-at-home type? Are you an Anglican, a Baptist, a Methodist, charismatic-liberal-evangelical something or other?

>Do you know? Do you care? Does it matter?

NOW READ 1 CORINTHIANS 3:1–9

Immerse

When I was at university and a part of the CU, the biggest issue seemed to be whether you were spiritual enough. Spiritual Christians went to the missionary prayer meeting before lectures, had a quiet time every day for more than an hour, handed out tracts on campus and held evangelistic pancake parties for people in their halls. Worldly people went to parties instead of CU meetings, and drank beer instead of grapefruit juice and lemonade. Now I look back and think what a load of baloney that was. Why did we put so much value on such superficial things?

>These new Christians at Corinth had probably been converted from pagan cults that worshipped the goddess Aphrodite. Corinth was a pretty immoral place and so it was a huge change for them to now live by Christian standards of sexual purity and faithfulness. All through the letter, Paul reminds them to look to Jesus to see how they should live.

Re-engage

Paul tells the Corinthians that they need to be more spiritual – but he doesn't mean that other-worldly, detached-from-reality, impress-people-with-how-many-meetings-you-go-to stuff. What were the signs that they were being worldly (verses 3 and 4)? What did he think it meant to be spiritual?

>How important to you are the labels you wear as a Christian – are you covered in spiritual logos? Perhaps the denomination you belong to? The festivals you go to? The type of Bible you use or music you listen to? It's great to find a place to feel at home, a community to belong to, things that help you in your faith. But are you wearing labels instead of following Jesus?

Airlock: Becoming

DIY SOS

Themes: Lifestyle, Good works

Decompress

All together now boys and girls, let's sing:
'The wise man built his house upon the rock,
the wise man built his house upon the rock,
the wise man built his house upon the rock,
and the rains came tumbling down.
The rains came down...'
Go on, do the actions – no one's looking!

NOW READ 1 CORINTHIANS 3:10–23

Immerse

I love watching DIY programmes. Not just to drool over the finished rooms, but because I love to marvel at the DIY mess that some people live in. I hate to stereotype, but it's usually the blokes who enthusiastically knock down walls, or rip out kitchens, and then never get round to replacing them. And then it's down to the women in their lives to nag, sulk and finally ring up the TV producers to try and shame them into doing something about it, or get the experts in to sort it out for them. What I want to know is why don't the women just get on and do it themselves instead of moaning?

> On first reading, this passage can sound a bit like 'make sure you do good things so you get saved' – surely the opposite of what it means to be a Christian? Paul is talking here to people who would already count themselves as Christians. They have already decided that they want to base their lives on Jesus – to build their house upon the rock so to speak – and so Paul is asking them to think about the kind of house they want to build on the foundation of Christ. Or in other words, now you belong to Christ, what is your life going to be like? It's your choice.

Re-engage

Imagine your life as if it was a house. Which rooms or areas of your life are looking good – smart, sorted and comfortable to be in? Which rooms need a bit of work – maybe they're cluttered, or need some old stuff taken out? Invite Jesus to walk around your life, and show you what he would build differently. You could draw your life like a house floor plan, with different rooms representing different areas of your life.

Airlock: Becoming

Themes: Judging, Criticism

Superstars in the stocks

Decompress
Think about your church leader or youth leader. When did you last criticise them? When did you last say something positive about them?

NOW READ 1 CORINTHIANS 4:1–5

Immerse
Recent shows like *Pop Idol* and *Fame Academy* have given the world a brand new batch of pop stars. The trouble is, they only have a limited appeal. Once the TV exposure runs out, so does the positive press coverage, and the adulation and chart success slowly disappears. And then they're left washed up at the age of 20. Whatever you might think of their music, their talent and their choices, it seems the criticism they receive is as over the top as the initial euphoria when they begin. They're only pop stars after all.

>In today's passage, Paul continues his theme of how Christians should view their leaders. He's already said that they're only doing their job and they're not to be followed like superstars. Now he addresses some of the super-critical Corinthians who have been bad-mouthing the apostles.

Re-engage
I think it's all too easy for us to put Christian leaders on pedestals and treat them like superstars, or else put them in the stocks and pelt them with criticism. In verse 2, what quality does Paul say leaders need to have above everything else? Who is the ultimate judge of a leader (v 4)?

>Think about Christian leaders that you relate to. Do you tend to put them on a pedestal or in the stocks?

>Think of something you could do to encourage your church leader, your youth leader, your house-group leader or any other flavour of leader you may have. This could be sending them an email, writing them a thank you note, buying them a bar of chocolate, praying for them or telling them what you appreciated about the last service they led – or think of something else. And then do it!

Airlock: Becoming

Themes:	Pride, Leadership,

Suffering for the gospel

Decompress

Think of the person who is, in your opinion, the best advert for the Christian faith – someone who lives it out and really knows God. What words would you use to describe them?

NOW READ 1 CORINTHIANS 4:6–21

Immerse

Some celebrities demand to be treated as if they are royalty. They expect red-carpet treatment, the right brand of mineral water in their dressing room, accommodation and freebies for all their friends and families etc. But they're not all like that. David Schwimmer is best known for playing the part of Ross in *Friends*. In spite of being paid hundreds of thousands of dollars per episode, he doesn't demand star treatment. If he's waiting for coffee in Starbucks and gets invited to the front of the queue just because of who he is, he insists on waiting his turn. 'I find it sad that everyone wants their fifteen minutes of fame and, in America, we're so consumed by it,' he says.

Re-engage

It's not just celebrities who expect star treatment. Obviously the Corinthians were very full of themselves and feeling proud of how they were doing in their Christian life. Paul wanted them to realise what it's like to be a leader – not glamorous or easy. Look at the words Paul uses to describe his own situation in verses 9 to 13. Hardly a good advert for Christianity – or is it? What makes it worthwhile for Paul (vs 14,15)? The Corinthians were very full of themselves; Paul was full of Jesus Christ and the challenge of making him known.

> Paul calls himself the Corinthians' father in Christ, because he was the one who told them about Jesus. Acts 18:1–11 tells how Paul started teaching the Jews in Corinth, but when they wouldn't accept what he said, he went next door to talk to the Gentiles. He stayed in the city for a year and a half, supporting himself by working as a tentmaker with two friends that he made, Priscilla and Aquila.

> Remember the person you thought about at the start? Find out how much their life has been like Paul's – hard work but worth it. Write to them, email, ring them up or just go round for a chat. What advice would they give you when the going gets tough?

Airlock: Becoming

Themes: Purity, Discipline

Life laundry

Decompress
It only takes one sock, one black sock, to sneak into a white wash when no one is looking and it happens. Everything turns grey.

NOW READ 1 CORINTHIANS 5:1-13

Immerse
I recently watched an episode of *Life Laundry*, the home improvement show where two presenters turn up and help someone unclutter their homes and dejunk their lives. In this particular episode, Dave was being confronted by his wife Alison about his habit of collecting things – Ladybird books, soda siphons, pottery. He loved going to car boot sales and getting bargains, but the problem was that he wasn't very discerning. He'd buy any old junk, even if he already had something like it, and it was gradually spilling out of his study and filling every spare corner of the house. He and Alison had to make do with a cardboard box full of clothes in their bedroom, because the wardrobe was full of his collections! But all credit to him, he went through the painful process of chucking out tons of his beloved stuff – and it probably saved his marriage. It certainly made his house look a lot better.

Airlock: Becoming

> Is there anything in your life that you need to get rid of?

Re-engage
It seems like Paul is being quite harsh here, but it shows how important holiness and purity were to him. And how important it was that the Corinthians were different to the people in the town – but not by doing worse things than them, which is what had just happened! If nothing was done about this incest what message would that give to the Christians in the church and to those non-Christians outside? Was this a loving way to react? Paul has told the Corinthians to be united in chapter 1. Now he tells them to keep away from people in the church who sin (v 11).

> Is he contradicting himself?
> If you feel you have done something wrong and it hasn't been dealt with – you haven't said sorry, or don't feel forgiven – talk to a Christian friend about it, or just pray by yourself. Don't leave it to fester and infect other parts of your life.

Bake a cake or a loaf of bread. Use a packet mix if you like. Make something with yeast or self-raising flour in it so that it rises. And as you wait for it to cook, and the delicious smells fill the kitchen, sit and pray. Ask God to show you where there's sin in your life that, like yeast, is in danger of spreading and taking over. Ask him to wash you clean.

Extra_1 Mark 8:14–21
Extra_2 Luke 13:18–20

Themes: Evangelism, Forgiveness

Outrageous plans

Decompress

A man takes an adulterous woman for a wife. The couple have a child and choose a name like 'Unloved'. The woman starts seeing another man with better olive oil, grain and facial hair. The husband gets angry and rebukes his adulterous wife… Sounds like a soap opera doesn't it?

NOW READ HOSEA 3:1–5

Immerse

An American evangelist once saw two young teenage prostitutes looking for customers on a street corner in New York. He asked the girls how much it would cost to hire them both for a night. He paid the girls and booked a hotel room. Then he disappeared out to a local video shop in the area… He came back with children's videos and some food. They spent the evening watching the films, laughing and joking like the children that they should have been allowed to be.

>Imagine the great risks that the evangelist took – the compromising position he put himself in. Think about how the girls would have felt afterwards. But also look carefully at how God showed his love for his people through the evangelist. Even today, God asks outrageous things of his prophets in the world…

Airlock: Becoming

Re-engage

How would you feel if God told you to make up with someone who had betrayed you and then flaunted their betrayal in front of your friends? Not only did Hosea have to break Old Testament law to carry out God's will, but he also had to suffer the humiliation of paying Gomer's toyboy to get her back – was she really worth that? God thought so!

>Yet notice the way that Hosea strikes a two-way bargain that includes his purity as well as hers (v 3). Hosea has no need to accept any of the responsibility for the collapse of his relationship with Gomer, yet he has the humility to include himself in the solution. What does this show us about God's love for us, and how we could bring God into our confrontations? Hosea's willingness to sacrifice himself allows God an opportunity to communicate with his people in an acutely powerful way that is irresistible to the Israelites – through human example.

>If God's command to you is not 'Go Show Love To A Prostitute' then what is it? What outrageous plan does God have for you? Pray that he will enable you to build up your strength and that you will know the right time to take a risk and make a difference to the lives of many!

Case for the prosecution

Themes: Unfaithfulness, Sin

Decompress

Your breath smells, you look like a dog and you ought to wash more often. If you can't take criticism, then you're going to struggle with the next few pages. But whilst my criticism is based on my rude and obnoxious nature, God's criticism is based on him being an all-knowing, all-seeing kind of guy. So listen up…

NOW READ HOSEA 4:1–3

Immerse

My local newspaper contains numerous reports on killing and stealing. The national newspapers are full of stories of adultery. At school this week (I'm a teacher), I have dealt with incidents involving swearing, lying and stealing (fortunately no killings or adultery just yet). And people say that the Bible is irrelevant!

>The world is trapped in a seemingly unending circle of sin and depravity, and you and I are just as responsible as anyone else. In fact, as Christians we are more responsible, because there are 'those in the land who do not know God'. Face it – until we treat our God with a bit more loyalty and respect, the hope that Jesus has given us lies forgotten and unknown by the very people he came for.

Re-engage

This passage tells us some home truths about why things have gone so wrong. 'How can you expect a sin-free world,' asks God, 'when you treat me like I don't exist?' (see v 1). The qualities that God wants in us are 'loyalty' and 'truth'. In our lives, what would be the consequences of us being loyal and true to God? What sort of things would we have to change?

>The sickness of the world is caused by sin (v 3) and in particular, 'cursing, killing, lying, stealing and adultery'. How many of us can live a week without putting someone else down? Without trying to wriggle our way out of trouble by lying? Without letting lust control our words and actions?

>Yes, Lord, we stand guilty. And yes, Lord, we need help.

>God's case for the prosecution is watertight. We know that we stand condemned. And yet I have a feeling that God wants us to focus on 'loyalty' and 'truth' rather than sin. Do you want to see the people who you love turn to God? Relax – you have the same desire as God. Now try to put it into practice. Pray that God will show you the way of truth over the coming days.

Airlock: Becoming

Themes: Evangelism, Sin, Prayer

Who's to blame?

Decompress

I think I've been casting God wrong in the motion picture that goes through my head whenever I'm reading the Bible. For so long, I've had God's voiceover full of venom and anger. I think perhaps it might be time to let someone else take over. What type of voice do you think God is using?

NOW READ HOSEA 4:4–11

Immerse

Just try a little experiment – read the passage again, replacing the word 'priests' with 'Christians' and 'people' with 'non-Christians'. Now I'm not trying to say that all Christians are all heretics bound for hell! But this will give you a bit more of an idea of what God means here. The priests in Hosea's time were running around telling the people they were naughty, but weren't offering any meaningful guidance.

>Ever given friends advice on a variety of issues including who and who not to go out with, how far to go sexually and who to hang about with? How often do we mention God? Do we make ourselves feel better or our friends? Are we setting people free from the law, or are we being God's Gestapo?

Re-engage

'Don't stand there clicking your tongue and disapproving of non-Christians if you're not prepared to guide them!' (see vs 4,5). That would be an interpretation of God's message to the church today.

>Here's some good news – you should never feel uncomfortable about praying for non-Christians, whether they know about it or not. But if you're going to pray, then you're going to have to say or do something about it sooner or later, because if the people never receive any knowledge, then they are lost (v 6).

>Those of us who are still mastered by sin are not fully living as God's people (v 7). We can be of little use to others – after all, why would a drowning person cling on to a sinking ship? And the consequences of sinking are harsh and dire (v 9) – we would do well to remember this!

>We need to pray for an uncompromising attitude in our lives, so that we can at least be a rock in a stormy sea, waiting for the lifeboat to save us and all those who cling to Jesus through us. Is there anything specific that is making you sink? Ask God to remove the weight from around your neck and help you float.

Airlock: Becoming

Themes: Unfaithfulness, Sin

All aboard the stupid bus

Decompress
Newsflash! Newsflash! God in sarcastic irony shock! Prepare for some divine dark humour… with some vital nuggets of truth!

NOW READ Hosea 4:12–19

Immerse
One of my favourite 'teacher catchphrases', used by one of my colleagues at school, is 'Ding ding! All aboard the stupid bus!' And I think sometimes it's important for us to realise that as Christians we can still find ourselves on the wrong bus…

>My colleague uses this catchphrase as a good-humoured way of getting pupils to concentrate and focus on the task in hand. And that is exactly the tone that God is using in the first part of this passage – almost like a comedian reflecting on the ridiculous nature of the world.

>But like all good comedy, the basis of these verses lay in the accuracy of the observation. And like the best comedy, it is based in tragedy – the overwhelming stupidity of God's people. Do you get a sense of God's frustration in these verses? Because when the laughter stops, there's some serious thinking to do.

Re-engage
For all the common sense in this passage, it can sometimes seem like we're stuck in a God-forsaken reality TV programme – *I'm A Christian: Get Me Out Of Here*. It is so blindingly obvious that some of our idols are completely useless, but the harshness of the world that we are in can make quick fixes seem appealing. Don't be fooled, though – because the sin bus will eventually pull into to 'shame-town', no matter how long the journey takes.

>It's time to be really honest. What do we feel is in the power struggle in our minds to take our attention away from God? How can we overcome it?

>Remember how hard it must have been for the Israelites to tear themselves away from the idols. Some of these things are going to be so hard to let go. Keep on praying, identify your idols and smash them.

Airlock: Becoming

Themes: Evangelism, God's anger

Urgent assistance required

Decompress

OK, today's passage might make some people 'quite cross'... God is about to reveal a bit of a mean streak – but it's all for our own good, so read on!

NOW READ HOSEA 5:1–15

Immerse

To start with, can I just point out that we are ALL sinners and we are ALL subject to all manner of temptations and desires. And sometimes we ALL need a good kick up the backside. Fair enough? Good.

>Sin has its consequences – it will always catch up with you and it will always lead to grief. Think about all the classic soap opera showdowns – built up by weeks of storylining and then BANG! – a punch-up or cat fight featuring the well-known phrases 'YOU SLAG!', 'YOU'RE NOT MY MOTHER!' and 'YOUR DOG WEED THROUGH MY LETTERBOX!'.

>But what happens after the showdown? A winding down, a licking of wounds. And it's the same for us when we reach the showdowns in our lives – the places where all our sin and bitterness catches up with us. And after the BANG! is where God can step in (if he hasn't already) and do some serious business...

Re-engage

Isn't it tempting to gloss over this passage and pretend that it's not here? Nasty God, and poor Israelites! After all, they'd only ignored their Creator and worshipped pieces of wood, and gone about stealing, committing adultery, lying...

>Of course, at this point I am thinking 'uh-oh'. I've been being an Israelite... (I must rid my house of pieces of wood and soon!) But does God have the right to kill me as a punishment?

>Through Jesus, we have been given a different way. We no longer incur God's wrath in such a powerful way, because Jesus deflected the anger from us on the cross. Yet there will be times when we go to worship God but we cannot find him (v 6). And that's when we need to start praying...

>Even if you are struggling with God's attack on the unbelievers, just remember that this is how he feels about people today. What will happen to those who do not have Jesus as their shield? Does this convey the urgency for evangelising and praying for your friends, because it should do! Think of one non-Christian and pray for them.

Airlock: Becoming

A poem for the questioners

There are whens and wheres I can't explain,
Whys I don't understand.
I'm not so hot on who or what
And whethers, buts and ands.
Yet I've burned with all these questions,
For your path is one I've trod,
And when you ask 'Why follow him?'
I can only say, 'Because'.

Because I know you're worth his sacrifice,
And that he delights in you.
Because I know when I come to glory,
I want you to enter too.
Because I know you're made in heaven,
And his stamp is plain to see,
And I know he loves you like I do,
So won't you walk with me?

Think about non-Christians that you love. What would be the best way to help them know God?

Extra_1 Matthew 28:16–20
Extra_2 2 Corinthians 4:1–6

Themes: Revenge, Retaliation

Payback

Decompress

'Dear Lord, the revenge thing. There are people in this world who I want to walk up to and hit. Hard. In the face. Give 'em a good bashing. For what they've done to me, to people I know, to people I don't know even. So how does the whole 'turn the other cheek' scenario work in these kinds of situations, Lord? Amen.'

NOW READ MATTHEW 5:38–42

Immerse

Turn the other cheek? If there's something that this world isn't keen on, it's saying, 'Hey, so you hit one side of my face. Why not try this side too?' And in some cases, that seems fair enough, doesn't it? If someone takes your family hostage, you're not about to say, 'Hey, brilliant, take me as well!' But should you?

>Religion isn't just used just as an excuse for violence, it's used as the reason. It grows, mutates, becomes something more than what it was when it began. The essence of the belief, the standards, the morals, become distorted, twisted, even forgotten. And all that's left is blindness, violence and uncompromise. It can happen between two people, two religions, two nations, a whole world. Everyone scrabbling to blame everyone else, when actually we are all to blame.

Re-engage

It's easy to look at others far off and say, 'Well, I can't see why they just don't stop the killing. It's not solving anything. It's just an eye for an eye and everyone's losing.' But just put yourself in their position. Think about what it's like – what they've suffered, what they believe, how long the battle's been going on for. Now do you understand? Turning the other cheek isn't as easy as it sounds. Which is what Jesus is saying. The problems go much deeper, right to the heart and soul of mankind.

>Got views on something that's going on in the world? Think you know it all? Think you've got all the answers? Well, you haven't. And to prove it to yourself, find out what the other side think, why they think it, why they do what they do and risk what they risk. Put yourself in their shoes. Only then can you have any notion of what 'understanding' means. Do some study on a conflict that is happening in the world today, perhaps the Israel/Palestine conflict. Why is it happening?

Airlock: Becoming

Themes:	Enemies, Love

Neighbours

Decompress

'Lord, I'm not sure how I'm supposed to love my enemies. I'd much rather punch them in the face, or at least talk about them behind their back. But that's not what you're after. You want me to love them. I think, Lord, I need to understand a little more about what you mean by 'love'. Amen.'

NOW READ MATTHEW 5:43–48

Immerse

There's someone you don't like, isn't there? No, I'm not talking about the person who did that thing that upset you just a little, or that group who you think probably said that about you because someone told you they did. I'm talking about THAT person. Yep, that's the one. The one who makes you angry; who makes your heart pump, your fists clench and every swear word you've ever heard pop into your brain.

>Hard to imagine loving them, isn't it? Much easier to imagine rubbing their face in wet grit. But that's not what Jesus is after. The command is simple – love your enemy. Love them. Now think about that word 'love'. What does it mean? That you like something? That you're passionate about something? Or is there more to it than that? Jesus died on the cross – a love thing. Died for people who we'd see as his enemy. That's real love. Got it yet?

>To get another handle on Jesus' view of loving your enemy, why not check out Luke 10:25–37, everyone's favourite, the good Samaritan? The Jews saw the Samaritans as nothing more than the dregs of humanity. So here, Jesus has the enemy of the Jews doing what God truly requires – showing love regardless of the situation.

Re-engage

So what's this passage telling you about your attitude to those people you simply can't stand? Do you really think you can look Jesus in the eye and act the way you do? Be honest. Be real. Jesus was/is both, and commands us to be nothing less than that also.

>OK, double dare time – start praying about that person you hate. Every night, get that person before God in your mind. Do this every night for a very, very long time.

Airlock: Becoming

Themes: Showing off, Sex, Image

That don't impress me much

Decompress
'Lord, I can't help it – sometimes I want people to know that I've done something good, something charitable. It's a mix of wanting to show off, a sense of feeling good about what I've done, and that urge to let others know so that they can pat me on my back. The only person I should really want to know what I've done is you, Lord. Help me sort this one out. Amen.'

NOW READ MATTHEW 6:1–4

Immerse
Ever get the impression that this is the world of the 'me'? Take a look around you and see what's being peddled as vitally important. It's not other people, that's for sure. It's you. That's what's up there with water and food as essential for a fulfilling life. Image. Doing it for yourself. Your future, your success, your everything. Me me me me me. You can even buy the T-shirt with that on it, as though it's now something which is desirable.

>This is the self society. Take sex as an example. It's no longer something to be shared between two people, something quite extraordinary that two people share in love. It's not even the free, do-it-all-anywhere sex from the sixties that we all hear about far too often. Instead, it's sex of the self. It's about your pleasure, your satisfaction. It's about finding someone who can make you feel good, who knows just how to please you, how to turn you on. It's got nothing to do with them anymore. Just you. That's all that matters. And if it's happened with sex, that most intimate and shared of experiences, what else can it happen with?

Re-engage
Think about it – Jesus probably got desperately annoyed with those people who just waltzed around in their wealth and their law, and then occasionally made a big deal about giving very little indeed to help the poor. So he makes it very clear that God simply isn't faffed about what other people think of you, just about what you think of you and your relationship with him. So if you do good, what does it matter if no one knows? Why should they? The good things you do should only be done because of who you are with God, not so that other people can see you.

>Join a charity. Give regularly. Don't let anyone know. Ever. This is between you and God and no one else. Till the day you meet him at heaven's gate.

Airlock: Becoming

Themes: Prayer, The Lord's Prayer

How to pray

Decompress

'Words are always difficult when I'm praying, Lord. Which is a bit of a problem, really. The last thing I want to be a problem is words if I'm speaking to you. But they are. Sometimes I just witter on and on and on, saying nothing. Other times I'm silent. Then occasionally, when I'm out walking, I'll say just what's on my mind and it all seems as so much more valuable. I need to get the balance right, Lord. Help me. Amen.'

NOW READ MATTHEW 6:5–15

Immerse

Everyone knows one. Everyone's heard one. And most people have wanted to shout at them to stop. Who are we talking about? Prayer gurus. The ones who, at every meeting, are desperate to lead everyone in prayer, pray for everyone, pray longer than everyone. It seems like all they're bothered about isn't actually the praying so much as the 'Look at me everyone! I'M PRAYING! Hear my words! Don't you wish you were like me, able to pray like me, just be me?' The answer we all have screaming in our head is 'Noooooooooooo!'

>But perhaps these people should make us look at ourselves a little bit closer. After all, why are we so bothered that these people pray the way they do? What does it matter? Surely we can't be jealous, can we? Can we?

Re-engage

The Lord's Prayer... Now there's something we don't use to full effect. OK, so we regularly recite it at church, but that's about it. Jesus meant it to be more than that. It's a prayer plan really. So why not use it? Why don't we take this amazing prayer and use it as the basis for our own prayer life? After all, so often we seem to find ourselves wondering what to say, what to think. Much simpler to use the prayer Jesus taught us, tie our own prayers into it, and get sorted, don't you think?

>It's easy, but it's quite a good exercise – write your own version of the Lord's Prayer. Use the 'plan' that Jesus has given us. Do this each night for a week. Then, look at everything you've written and see for yourself how following that simple structure has helped you focus your thoughts with God. Simple. Effective. Bit like Jesus' message really.

Airlock: Becoming

Themes: Fasting, Discipline

Fish 'n' chips

Decompress

'Me and food, Lord... Well, we're great mates. Food is a hobby and it's a tough one to take in hand and control. But I need to, Lord, and if I can control that bit of my life, then perhaps I've more of a chance with the rest of it? Amen.'

NOW READ MATTHEW 6:6–18

Immerse

Fast food. We assume it's fast and that if it's fast that means it's good. Well, most times it isn't all that fast. The queues go on forever, the service is nothing more than shouts and grunts, and rarely is your order ready instantly, but instead needs to be shouted to someone out of view strapped to a huge grill. Also, we assume it's food, and that can be a lie, can't it? But then it's so easy to forget that food should be good for you, and that it should have some nutritional value and shouldn't all taste dull and bland.

>But man cannot live by junk food alone, even if it does come with onion rings. So what are we going to do? Live a life with no change, bland food, bland everything? Or are we going to take control, make a change, expect (perhaps even demand) taste in our food, and substance in our abstinence, in everything?

Re-engage

Fasting. Is it a good thing? Well, yes, and it's not just a case of giving up chocolate at Lent. Taking control of your eating helps you focus on what's going into your body. Before you know it, you're thinking beyond that and looking at not just physical food, but spiritual food. You've got a handle on keeping your physical self healthy and well fed, now you can get focused on keeping your spiritual self healthy and well fed. Simple, eh?

>Three choices:

>One: Next time you have the urge to hit the burger bar, turn around and walk away, then with the money you would've spent, use half of it to buy something healthy to eat, and the other half of it give to the guy sitting at the entrance to the shopping centre, in the dirty clothes and the old sleeping bag.

>Two: What are you thinking? Why do you need that rubbish inside you? Why not take control of what you eat, get involved, cook something, enjoy your food, love it, live it, eat it. Sorted.

>Three: Fast, as per the instructions in Matthew 6:16–18

Airlock: Becoming

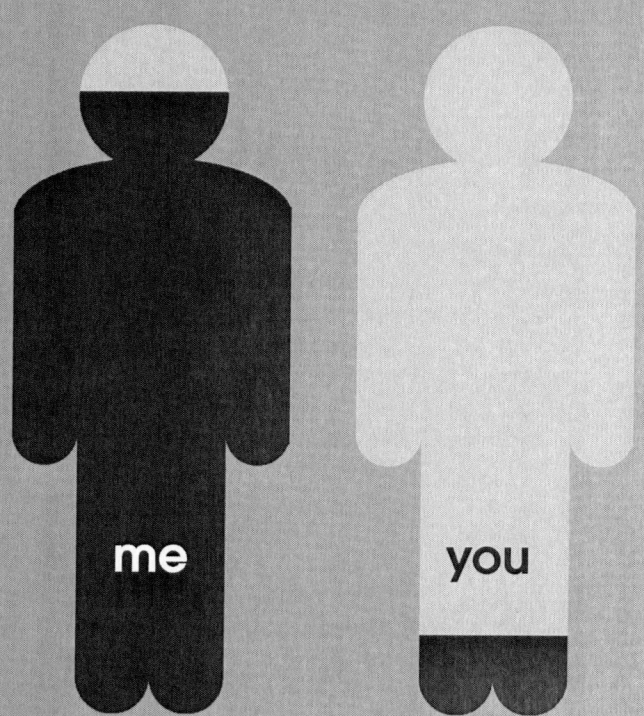

Have you ever heard of tithing? It's when you give ten per cent of your earnings to charity. It was something that people did in the Old Testament, and it's still something that churches like to encourage today.

If you think God is challenging you about the way you spend your money, start now and make it a regular habit. Look at it this way – you make £20 a week from that job in the chemists – so that's only £2 a week you don't get but someone else does. Good, eh? You could give the money to your church, or club together with some friends and sponsor a child overseas...

Extra_1 **Leviticus 27:30–33**
Extra_2 **Deuteronomy 12:1–6**

Themes: Promises, Miracles, Belief

Mother impossible

Decompress
Have you ever found it difficult to believe God's promises? Has a particular personal situation ever led you to think that God can't act? Pray – Lord, help me believe and trust in your promises because you are faithful.

NOW READ GENESIS 18:1–16

Immerse
I live in Essex, and although I don't wear white stilettos, nonetheless I feel it's my duty to know what I should, or more importantly should not, be wearing. It seems though that this summer, THE accessory to have, was utterly unavailable to me – having a bump. Being pregnant is so 'now, darling!'. Madonna has done it, Gwyneth Paltrow has done it… and even, shock horror, one of my best friends is pregnant! Now logically, I know it's possible for me to be pregnant because I'm a woman. But for me, at the moment, it the most unbelievable thing that could happen. Could a child really, really, really grow inside me?

>David Blaine does some amazing tricks – prior to him being inside a huge glass box for weeks and weeks, I would have said it was completely impossible and it couldn't be done. It's difficult for something to be really impossible, yet still happen, unless God is involved. Sarah, Abraham's wife was around 90 years old. It seemed imposible that she could ever have a child, but God said it was possible, and it was going to happen. And it did.

Re-engage
Sarah becoming pregnant at the age of 90 seems like an impossible feat. Sarah reacted in a way I imagine most of us would if we were told something impossible was about to happen to us – she laughed. How many times do we not believe or mock God's promises? Do you limit God to what is humanly possible, or are you willing to believe that God can do more than we could ever ask or imagine (see Ephesians 3:20)?

>Start (or continue) writing down your prayers in a journal, listing everything you pray for. God will act over time and you will be amazed as to how he answers your prayers. Prepare to believe that God can do anything.

Airlock: Becoming

Themes: Prayer, Justice, Promises

If only...

Decompress

Thank God for all that he has provided. Even if your life doesn't seem great at the moment, he makes the sun come up every day, he created beautiful places for us to see and he created us. Think back to the last time you asked for something in prayer. Did it happen?

NOW READ GENESIS 18:17–33

Immerse

I went to university in Canterbury and studied Business and Religious Studies (a funny combination, I know, but it's good for my job now!). I spent many nights on my knees praying, 'Lord, please help me with this essay… I promise I'll be good!' We all do this from time to time. Some Christians call this an arrow prayer, which usually means 'Lord, get me out of this fix, quick!'

>Sometimes I got OK grades, sometimes really good grades. But my marks usually related to how much reading and work I had put into that particular assignment. Prayer is like having a conversation with God. But I wonder how many times our prayers appear to be more of a shopping list of 'I wants' than a dialogue between humanity and God?

>In today's passage, Abraham is desperate to help his nephew, Lot, who lives in Sodom, so he pleads with the Lord.

Re-engage

Abraham knows how to pray. In this passage, he prays for Lot and his family, and presumably other people in Sodom and Gomorrah who weren't really bad people. Look again at verse 25 – Abraham knows that God is a fair God and will always do right, so pleads through his knowledge of the character of God that he would not destroy the righteous alongside the wicked.

>We can learn from Abraham, as he appeals to the Lord on the basis that God is just and fair. When we pray, do we simply pray for what we want or do we trust that God is good and righteous and will be just? Sometimes it is difficult to see how God will act, or if he can. But God is in control, and can see the bigger picture.

>Make it your mission to pray in the knowledge of the character of God. Note down from this reading some of God's key characteristics and remember them!

>Write them on a large piece of paper and stick it on the wall next to your posters of pop stars.

Airlock: Becoming

Themes: Moral decisions, Evil

The decision is yours

Decompress
Try to remember the last big decision you made. What things influenced you to make your choice? Maybe your family, friends or even the media had a hand in how you decided. Do you think these things are a good influence on how you make decisions?

NOW READ GENESIS 19:1–11

Immerse
It was my birthday recently, and my brother gave me an extra funky set of cutlery – I was chuffed. Believe it or not, a small instruction book was supplied with the cutlery. What's more, I read it and it said that although the cutlery was dishwasher proof, if it stayed in the cutlery basket with cutlery made from different metal, it could cause my groovy new bits of cutlery to become discoloured and stained. After reading this helpful little book, I promptly put my new cutlery in the dishwasher with my old cutlery, and forgot about it as I left to go away for a few days. When I got back, I opened the dishwasher to find that my old cutlery had gone rather crusty and green, and my new cutlery all dark and blotchy. I then remembered the little book of instructions. I had mixed stainless steel cutlery with silver cutlery.

>Noticing what's around you is important, if you want to stay different and not go green and crusty.

Re-engage
I really can't imagine what was going through Lot's mind when he decided to offer his daughters to the mob of men outside his house. Maybe as the men of the town requested sex with his male visitors, Lot thought that offering women would turn the angry crowd away. Maybe hospitality customs were so particular, that this seemed like his only option. For whatever reason, by living and not remaining separate enough from society and its morals, Lot thought in this awful way. Does your culture, your friends and your family affect you? Are you able to stand up for God? If not, why not?

>Write down a list of influences on your most recent decision. Do you think they are the best influences to help you make good decisions that give God a good name? If not, why not change them today? Jesus talks about simply cutting out what causes you to do things that are wrong (see Mark 9:43).

Airlock: Becoming

| Themes: | Obedience, Sin, Future |

Don't stop moving

Decompress

Take a piece of paper and chart the ups and downs of your spiritual life, noting the things that have altered your spiritual journey. Thank God that each event has helped you become the person you are, and pray that you might learn from your past and look to your future.

NOW READ GENESIS 19:12–22

Immerse

I went on my first date when I was 12. The date was set for Saturday afternoon, so I made my dad drive to South Woodford cinema, where I saw *My Girl 2*, with my new boyfriend. I say a date, but actually there was a group of eight of us who all went to the cinema together. I am sorry to tell you that our relationship didn't last for very long. In fact, I don't remember speaking to him for the next month! After we split up, I can remember thinking sometimes, 'Oh I wish I could go out with him again!' It was only when I stopped thinking in that way that I eventually found a new boyfriend. Constantly looking back over stuff that has happened doesn't help you move forward.

Re-engage

Lot has just been told by his visitors that Sodom is about to be destroyed and that he must flee the city, and now he faces two problems. Firstly, his closest family members, who he wants to take with him, don't believe what he says (v 14). And secondly, he begins to dither (v 16). Lot was so content with his culture, that he could not really appreciate the danger that the angels warned him of, but was fully aware of all that he would leave behind. It's easy to be critical of Lot, but how often do we look back, rather too longingly, on something that we know isn't good for us, perhaps something in our lifestyle? It is more difficult to obey God if we have become consumed by our culture. Do you live your life looking back at the silly things you have done, wishing and dreaming of a chance to do them again? Or do you look forward to God's plan for your life?

>Read Matthew 6:24. Jesus says that you cannot serve two masters so you have to decide to follow God's way or not. Have you looked back on something in your past a bit too much? Bring that situation to God in prayer. Ask him for new direction and freedom from it. Run as you are following God, looking forward and not back.

Airlock: Becoming

| Themes: | Disobedience, Hope |

Don't look back

Decompress

Try and remember the last time you broke a rule? What was it? Was it a sensible thing to do? Pray for the next time you are tempted to break an important rule – that you might do what is right and honouring to God.

NOW READ GENESIS 19:23–29

Immerse

When you see a 'do not walk on the grass' sign, what do you do? I confess the rebel in me just wants to walk on the grass. Or what about the ridiculously large, red button with a sign that says 'whatever you do, do not press'? I always want to press it. God told Adam and Eve that they could eat anything in the garden apart from the fruit of the tree of knowledge. So Adam and Eve ate that fruit (Genesis 3:1–7).

>Why are we like this? Why do we always want to disobey the rules? When my parents used to say, 'You have to be in by 10.30pm,' I used to think it was really unfair and that I had terribly uncool parents. But actually I realise now that they chose to set that rule because they loved me, knew what was best for me and wanted to protect me.

Re-engage

The destruction of Sodom and Gomorrah shows us that God doesn't tolerate sin. God is powerful and we must respect him. Lot's wife knew that she shouldn't look back but she did – she failed to recognise God's power and real anger towards the sin of Sodom that she was looking back to. Lot's wife didn't realise that God's command not to look back was for her protection. But God is not just waiting with a big bazooka to destroy sinners wherever he finds them. God loves us all deeply because he is our Father. Jesus mentions Sodom and Gomorrah in Luke 17, where he warns us that judgement is coming. Thankfully we can face God, as through Jesus dying for us, all our sins will be forgiven. Jesus offers new hope and freedom from all the wrong things in our lives.

>If you knew you had just one day until God came again, what would you spend it doing? Would you be more open with your friends about God, and why it's important to believe in Jesus, as he is the only way to heaven (John 14:6)? Pray that God will give you opportunities to share your faith with your friends (Colossians 4:2–6).

Airlock: Becoming

Extra B/21-25

If God told you to leave your community, friends, job and only take your family with you – would you be able to leave straight away? What would you struggle to leave behind?

**Ruth 1:1-22
Luke 18:18-25**

Themes: Holy Spirit, Tongues

Nutters

Decompress
'Dear Lord,
Fill me with your Holy Spirit;
Give me the words to say;
Be with me this day.'

NOW READ ACTS 2:14–21

Immerse
I don't know what kind of church services you go to. I've been to some over the years where bizarre things have gone on. People falling over, leaping up and down, shouting, laughing, making animal noises – and that was just the band.

>The Holy Spirit had descended on the disciples. They'd all spilled out onto the street after the tongues of fire and mighty wind stuff, babbling away in different languages and making quite a disturbance. Some of the crowd were amazed, hearing unschooled Galileans address them in their native tongues. Some onlookers reckoned they were drunk.

>So Peter addresses the crowd. He immediately aligns himself with them. 'Fellow Jews...' he calls them, and refers to Joel's prophecy, which the Jews would have believed to be totally credible, to draw in his amazed, but possibly puzzled or even alarmed audience, and reassure them that God was at work.

Re-engage
What is your response to scenes like this? I'm a pretty quiet kind of guy and I often find this sort of thing (and much less extreme stuff) difficult. I remember catching sight of someone bouncing around like a ball once. It was really embarrassing. Only thing was it turned out to be one of my pals. Believe me, he is not the sort of person who would normally show any sign of exuberance and would do anything to avoid looking – how shall I put it – like a complete prat.

>We've got to be careful of judging by appearances, though. Sure, some people get all excited in church and say and do crazy things, and it's sometimes not really anything to do with the Holy Spirit. But God looks at our hearts. Maybe the quiet guy in the corner is really doing the business with God. Maybe it's the weirdo swinging from the light fittings. Who knows? Look at your own heart. Most of the people on dancefloors on a Saturday night look nuts. It's just that that's become culturally acceptable.

>Make a concerted effort to be open to the Holy Spirit. Let him prompt you to do and say the things that God wants you to do and say.

Airlock: Becoming

Themes: Walking with God, Joy

Walking the walk

Decompress

'Lord, sometimes it feels like you are not there;
I look around but can't find you.
Help me keep you before me,
To focus on you; there in front of me;
Your arms open, your face welcoming.'

NOW READ ACTS 2:22–28

Immerse

Do you reckon you have a hard time? Demanding crowds always surrounded Jesus. He had no home, no financial security, no partner, had to deal with death threats, was in the constant presence of twelve numbskulls he was trying to disciple and was fully aware that he was going to die a painful, premature death. The only way he could keep it all together was to sneak off at five in the morning to find some time with God.

>Peter develops his argument here. There was no debate as to whether Jesus existed – he'd only recently been crucified. Peter refers to David – whose authority would have been unquestioned by the assembled Jews – to convince them that God had raised him from the dead.

>Peter quotes Psalm 16:8–11 which has, I reckon, some vital keys for fruitful, purposeful living.

Re-engage

In psalm 16, David describes Jesus as always keeping God before him, like walking towards a beacon, towards the light. This gave him his direction in life, the road he should follow. Because of this he had a continual awareness of God's presence by his side and knew he wouldn't be hurt or 'shaken' as it says in the NIV. We've all been hurt, but we can remain unshaken from our course whatever happens.

>Keeping God before him meant he was glad, and rejoiced. He was happy in other words, despite all the grief.

>So remember. Keep God before you. Nurture an awareness of his continual presence with you. If you can manage this, you'll stay on course despite life's knocks, and stay happy. Good, eh?

>Why not write out the words from this Psalm and keep them with you, in a pocket, pencil case, wallet, purse or as a desktop picture and keep God before you!

Airlock: Becoming

Dynamic duo

Themes: Evangelism, Worship

Decompress
'Lord, give me the strength to learn, share, break bread and pray with my Christian family.'

NOW READ ACTS 2:29-42

Immerse
The best communicators and teachers are those who can explain something to you in a way that you understand. A concept may be completely alien to you, yet by the time they have finished explaining it all, it is obvious.

>Peter develops his argument. He continues to refer to the accepted authority of the Old Testament and David's writings, to try and convince the Jews that Jesus had not only been killed but had been resurrected and was now pouring out the Holy Spirit – hence all the mayhem in the streets. When enough people were convinced that Jesus was Lord, he gave an appeal for submission to Christ.

Re-engage
This is what working in partnership with God's about. Peter uses everything at his disposal to win the crowd over. Humour, logical argument, empathy with the people...

>If you want your friends to know God, don't just present them with Christian clichés. What's going to really get them thinking? What's going to engage and provoke them? What are the questions you're going to have to answer before they'll even contemplate listening to you?

>On the other hand don't just talk at them. Pray God'll be 100% with you and anoint what you do.

>You want to lead worship? Don't expect God to use you if you've only just mastered C, G and D7 on your Argos six string and the only song you've learnt is 'She'll be comin' round the mountain when she comes'. Conversely, if all your effort goes into wowing the congregation with your new tune using 23 chords and 3 different keys, but you effectively said goodbye to Jesus when you walked out your door and all you're doing is showing off whilst the Holy Spirit's floating up near the rafters somewhere, you ain't going to cut it either.

>You know what I'm getting at.

>Let's pray as if God's got to do all the work and act as if we've got to do all the work.

>It's the same in everything we do – exams for example. Don't just pray you'll pass, learn your stuff.

Airlock: Becoming

The real deal

Themes: Christian living, Holiness

Decompress

What can I say? Today's passage is totally humbling. This is what it's about. This is how to do it. Nothing more to be said. End of story…

>What? I'm contractually bound to provide more than 28 words? Oh, OK then.

NOW READ ACTS 2:43–47

Immerse

Do we see loads of signs and miracles? No, not really. Do we live a non-materialistic lifestyle where others' needs are just as important as ours? Nope. Do we meet with other Christians on a daily basis and share food with joyful hearts? Well… kind of. I'm happy to see my Christian pals, although not that nutcase who sits at the back with the Millets windcheater, sandals and socks. And I don't mind sharing a meal. As long as it hasn't got onion in. Or spinach. And it doesn't taste anything like any of the stuff my mother used to make. Are we liked by all people? Are we seeing people saved every day? Er… next question?

>The believers met at both the Temple and their homes. This reminds us that church is not just four walls (or columns in the case of the Temple) but a community – it is us, the bride of Christ.

Re-engage

I doubt that any of us are quite where these guys were at this time. (We can look at other groups of believers in the New Testament and see a different story – the church at Corinth for example.)

>The thing is, let's start where we are and go forward. We aren't going to get there in one step. But let's pray our hardest, work our hardest, push forward and batter down any doors that stand in the way of us really doing the business with God. It's not something that is going to happen overnight, and it may be something that doesn't happen at all, but it's something to aim for, right? And the results of living such a lifestyle are clear to see – new believers were being added every day (v 47)!

>How can we stimulate not just us, but our churches, to live closer to this New Testament model? How about agreeing with a friend on one thing you can do to take you a step nearer to this kind of living?

Airlock: Becoming

Themes: Healing, Giving

Changing lives

Decompress
'Lord, show me what I can give to those who are in need.'

NOW READ ACTS 3:1-10

Immerse
What's your understanding of healing? Mine is that yes, God can intervene and heal people supernaturally. Only thing is I'm sitting here writing this with a frozen shoulder. Well, I'm actually writing this with a biro but you know what I mean. Anyway, this means I can't move my left arm properly and haven't been able to for some weeks. A few people have prayed for it but nothing much has changed. There's a bit of a gap between my belief and my experience at the moment. To be honest, I'm not in a place where I'd be happy to put my neck on the line like Peter and pray for God to heal someone else. I haven't got the faith for it and totally sympathise with anyone else who'd be reluctant to do what Peter did.

>I guess not too many of us have the guts to step out and put our faith on the line like this. This really is where the rubber hits the road. Either Peter's command 'Stand up and walk' works or it doesn't. Either he looks really cool or he looks a complete idiot:

'Errrr... ahem. Actually I was talking to someone else. Yes, I know it looked like I was talking to you but I've got a glass eye. See you around then.'

Re-engage
The crippled guy's life was totally changed after this encounter with Peter. The questions I ask myself are these. Whilst I'm waiting for my faith and knowledge and trust in God to grow in some areas, what are the things I can do in the meantime to change people's lives? Can I help someone through a problem? Can I bring a friend to a cell group or a service? Can I help someone financially? Can I bring some encouragement to someone? (And not just 'Yes, the black leggings and the knitted cardigan look great. No, really.') Of course if you've got faith and want to pray for healing for someone, good on you. Go for it.

>Peter hadn't got silver or gold. He gave what he could. What have you got that you can give? Most of us can't change the world. But we can change someone's world somewhere – go for it today.

Airlock: Becoming

What Bible passages point to our
need for the Holy Spirit in order to
achieve anything?

What passages point to our
responsibility to hard graft before
we see God work powerfully
in our lives?

Extra_1 John 14:15-31; 15:1-16
Extra_2 Philippians 3:1-11

| Themes: | Calling, Purpose, Reason |

What about me?

Decompress
What descriptions of God have you heard or read in the Bible? How relevant do you feel they are to you?

NOW READ ISAIAH 6:1–7

Immerse
Brown pants time. There you are, minding your own business in church, when all of a sudden, instead of the riot of acorns and bits of twig that Mrs Grunterling insists on calling a winter flower arrangement, you see the Almighty himself, in all his majesty, surrounded by all the heavenly host… Oh my!

>Except this probably hasn't happened to you. My first reaction is that I could do with this kind of guidance (although I would be a quivering pile of jelly on the floor if this did happen). I long to see the Lord, to hear what he says and to know what his plan for my life is, but so far, a thunderbolt like this hasn't happened to me. This is probably (alright, definitely) my fault, as I don't spend nearly enough time reading the Bible or praying.

>Isaiah knew that you would die if you came face to face with God, because of how unworthy humans are. (Moses and Jeremiah went through the same thing – see Exodus 3 and Jeremiah 1.) That's why he had to be purified. Although burning his lips might seem like an extreme method, lips were symbolic of the whole person (see also Leviticus 16:12 for similar imagery). But we don't have to go through this, because Jesus has done it for us. We can come to God whenever we want to, because Jesus has paid the price for our impurity.

Re-engage
God speaks to us all in a way that is relevant to us. He knows what would probably happen to me if I saw even a fraction of what Isaiah saw, but he is gracious enough to speak to me in a way I can understand, spiritual thicko that I am. All we need to do is spend time in his presence.

>How do you feel at the moment about God? Are you waiting for a dramatic vision of God himself? How much time do you actually spend with God?

>Put on some music, close the door, open your Bible and use this description of God to think about his majesty and splendour. Talk to him about his wonder and glory. Praise him!

Airlock: Becoming

Pick me!

Themes: Guidance, Obedience

Decompress

How quick are you to do something when a teacher or parent asks you to? Do you do it straight away or sit and moan until you have a huge fight about it?

NOW READ ISAIAH 6:8–13

Immerse

Look how ready Isaiah was to answer God's call:
>'Whom can I send?'
>'Ooh! Pick me! Pick me!'
>Hang on Isaiah, you don't even know what he wants yet. He might want you to become a Manchester United supporter, or go and work with someone who's just like David Brent. Don't be too hasty…
>Well, that's the point. Isaiah doesn't know what the Lord wants him to do and yet he still volunteers for it. How many times do we have important things to do but we never seem to get round to them - instead, we just sit there, whinging that 'I'm too tired. I've got a headache. I just want to finish watching *Neighbours*.' How much more do we resist if we know that it's going to be unpleasant or make us look a bit stupid (like actually telling someone that we're a Christian)?
>Isaiah said yes and found out that he wasn't going to do anything pleasant at all. He was going to have to speak to people who didn't want to listen, and to see Judah (his home) attacked and bullied by the countries around it. If we think God is telling us to do something, and we've prayed about it, then don't avoid it. Do it!

Re-engage

Look at verse 8 again. Look how freely Isaiah wants to obey God. If you were in the same position, what would your response be? Would you whinge and make excuses, or would you get up and do something? What is your attitude if you know you have to do something now? What should it be?
>What are you avoiding? Do you feel God has told you to do something? Well, here and now I suggest you go away and sort it out. You'll feel better when you've done it. Believe me, you will.

Airlock: Becoming

Gang warfare

Themes: Trusting in God, Friends

Decompress
Is there anyone making life difficult for you at the moment? Are any of them your friends?

NOW READ ISAIAH 7:1–9

Immerse
Friends can give you loads of grief sometimes – one minute you're the best of mates, the next you're at each others throats. Neighbours can be even worse (mind you, when I was a child, I was always a worse neighbour than anyone else – balls flying over fences, loud music blasting through the walls… what a nightmare we must have been).

>I have to confess that I don't really understand some of the fighting in the Old Testament and this confuses me even more. Israel and Judah were once one country, both following the Lord, both descended from Abraham, Isaac and Jacob. So why are they now fighting each other? Well, Israel and Syria wanted Judah to join in a pact against the powerful nation of Assyria, but the Lord warned Judah not join in. Ahaz, it seems, did have the stomach for a fight and joined with the Assyrians instead, watching their new big friends defeat Syria and Israel. Friendly…

>So Judah finds itself with two of its neighbours trying to attack Jerusalem, and Ahaz the king is bricking it somewhat. So would I. However, Isaiah comes with God's word. What is it?

>Well, Ahaz is told that the two attackers are weak and they won't succeed.

Re-engage
Why should this matter for you? Well, the chances are that if your mates are giving you a hard time, then they are as uncertain about life as you are. In fact they're more uncertain if they feel they have to take it out on other people to prove to themselves that they are in control.

>It's difficult to put up with, I'm not pretending it isn't, but trust God. If he can save whole cities from attack, then he's certainly there for you.

>'Love your enemies … pray for those who ill-treat you' (Luke 6:27).

>Think about anyone who is making your life difficult. Pray for them and for your relationship. Ask God to help you, then talk to others about what can be done. Don't try and cope with it on your own.

Airlock: Becoming

Mysterious ways?

Theme: God's ways

Decompress
Have you ever looked down on someone because they weren't a Christian? Did you ignore what they said, even though it might have been useful?

NOW READ ISAIAH 7:10–25

Immerse
Has anything happened to you that you didn't expect? I'm not talking about a check for five hundred pounds landing in your lap or suddenly finding yourself going out with the most attractive person you know. I mean more that someone (who is not a Christian) helps you in a significant way. Let me give you an example.

> I was once a teacher and shared a flat with a colleague who I really didn't like. He drank heavily, he slept with his students (sometimes more than one at a time) and, perhaps worst of all, he could only cook one meal, made of kidney beans, which looked like poo. After one late night episode (when he stood on the roof of the flats and peed into the street six storeys below), I couldn't cope and the only thing I could think of doing was to cry (literally) to God. The next day, our landlord (not a Christian) put him on probation and threatened to throw him out unless he apologised to everyone concerned.

> I really didn't know where help was going to come from, but God answered my prayer and used someone who was not a Christian to do it. The same was true for Ahaz, but he was not going to benefit from God using pagan countries. He was going to be humiliated because he wouldn't obey God (look at the beginning of the passage).

> God uses whoever he wants to put his plans into action, so don't reject help just because it comes from someone who doesn't know God. And if you need to be taught a lesson, God won't hesitate there either.

Re-engage
Think about all the people who you trust. How many of them aren't Christians? How much have they helped you? It can be very easy for us to think that help can only come from where we expect it to come, but the Bible is full of tales of the God using the unexpected.

> Is there something you need help with at the moment? Take it to God in prayer, but don't tell him how to sort it out – hand it completely over to him.

Airlock: Becoming

Themes: God's Word, Trust

Is there anyone at home?

Decompress
How quick are you to trust someone? Do you have to know them for ages before you value what they say?

NOW READ ISAIAH 8:1-10

Immerse
Some people never learn. As if Ahaz hasn't already been the biggest idiot on the planet, by ignoring God, refusing to obey him and generally being quite stupid, he still doesn't trust God's word. The people (including Ahaz) are still frightened of Israel and Syria, so he decides to bring in the Assyrians. He has replaced any trust he had in God with trust in the Assyrians, who are big and scary, and are quite obviously after anything they can get.

>Sometimes we don't like to think of God being judgmental and teaching his children a lesson, but sometimes that's what we need. Just as a mum will tell her children off for doing something stupid (running into the road, sticking their fingers into electric sockets) with the aim of both educating and rebuking the naughty child. It's just the same with God – sometimes he needs to tell us off for the same reasons.

>And let's face it, we can be as stupid and stubborn as little children if and when we want to be. Not trusting and obeying God, as Ahaz refused to do throughout his life, is one of the dimmest things of all.

Re-engage
Ahaz is described in both Kings and Chronicles as not walking in the ways of the Lord. What would the writer of Chronicles make of your life? How much would they be able to say about you trusting the Lord? It is one thing to say that we trust in the Lord but how much of that trust is displayed in the way we live and act?

>Is there something you know you should be (or shouldn't be) doing? Do you need help to overcome fear or embarrassment? Talk to someone you trust and pray about it. God will give you the strength to do whatever it is, be certain of that.

Airlock: Becoming

Should we just sit back, pray and let God do all the work? Or should we play our own part? Is prayer always the best course of action for any situation?

'Put your trust in God but keep your gunpowder dry!' Oliver Cromwell

Extra_1 Acts 12:1-19
Extra_2 James 5:13-18

| Themes: | Possessions, Money |

Money money money

Decompress

Think of the possession that you love the most. Become aware of how much you value it, treasure it. Remember all the pleasure that it has given you. Now give it away. Give it to someone who might need it, or if it's basically useless, sell it and give the money to someone who needs it. How does that feel? Just thinking about it? Now do you see what we're dealing with?

NOW READ MATTHEW 6:19-24

Immerse

I read something the other day by a brainy guy called John Gray. I don't know if it makes sense to you, but it sounds very brainy. He said that we are currently producing a new kind of celebrity, one who 'exchanges privacy for money'. There are lots of people today who seem to be famous for being famous – the *Big Brother* contestants perform in the human zoo and get their 15 minutes of fame.

>But is money really that great? Researchers at the University of Warwick recently claimed that winning as little as a thousand pounds would 'make our day', but the pleasure soon wears off. Of course these discussions prompt the usual replies: 'Money can't buy you happiness ... but it gets you a decent standard of misery.' Jesus is suggesting that Christians need to live by a different standard, something that people can see in our eyes... and no, I'm not talking about coloured contacts!

Re-engage

Where is your heart? It is a very simple question, but it cuts through all of our words, and all those songs we sing on a Sunday. It reveals the hypocrisy that Jesus had no time for. Where is your heart? If you are trying to follow Jesus but hoping he won't mind x, y and z in your life, you're better off not reading passages like this. Jesus says the 'worst darkness' comes from divided eyes – you think you're in the light, so you don't even think you need to seek the light. Sort it out!

>Go back and look at the Decompress section. Do you think you should do it? Talk to God about it. In some ways it might be more significant in our climate to give away something that can't be replaced, because we'll always have more money tomorrow... And if you are willing to show God that you're serious about him by holding your possessions lightly, then don't make a song and dance about it!

Airlock: Becoming

Themes:	Faith, Materialism

Don't worry, be happy

Decompress

Imagine that you are standing in front of a large trunk – the kind you see on station platforms in old black and white films. Put all the things that are bothering you in the trunk – words or objects that symbolise issues you are facing. Close the lid and put the case to one side. These problems aren't going to go away, but forget about them while you read today...

NOW READ MATTHEW 6:25–34

Immerse

In today's culture we're encouraged to have our futures mapped out precisely. It's one of the things that devout Muslims don't like about Christians. Muslims are taught to say 'Inshallah' before they do anything. It means 'if God wills it'. James 4:15 agrees with the Muslims on this one, but still we Christians have a tendency to take over our lives, such is our fear of the future.

>Nowadays, anyone who doesn't know what they're going to be doing in a year's time is either a spoilt student or a hopeless estate kid. Jesus takes a totally different tack (again!) – he suggests that the person who doesn't hassle themselves about tomorrow has the most hope, the most faith, the most direction...

>OK, so that's the obvious, spiritual bit. I'm struggling here, because as I write I'm wearing branded goods on all the parts of me that are covered, so I can't just reel off the stuff about trusting God for what I'm going to wear, because I'm not very good at it.

Re-engage

Trust is an underrated virtue in our culture. We assume that the people we meet are unreliable, and trusting them is going to get us hurt. Jesus speaks to us from a world in which God can be trusted, and he can be trusted, but as a doubter myself, I hunger for a time when I can know Jesus so well that I take him at his word and don't struggle. Jesus tells me to calm down and worry about the things that are happening to me right now.

>Why not try praying at the start of the day: 'God, I am wholly available to you. Let me see what you are doing and I will do it with you.' How about spending a day with no plans, maybe going to your local town with no money, and seeing what God might want to do with you. It might take a few hours to get out of the rhythm that ensnares us, but open yourself up to God...

Airlock: Becoming

Themes: Hypocrisy, Judging others

Christians are hypocrites

Decompress

Aren't people annoying? They let you down, they say one thing and then do another.

>Make a list of the things that really annoy you about people and ask yourself these questions: is this really something that I'm struggling with myself? Is it really my business? It is really worth hating someone over?

NOW READ MATTHEW 7:1-6

Immerse

Here Jesus sounds like your average cool dude who tells everyone that we should all just love each other and not criticise. 'Christians are always so judgmental, man! We should love and accept each other. That's what real love is, man!'

>Except of course that isn't what Jesus says at all. He suggests that it makes more sense to take the cack out of our own eyes before we start fiddling with someone else's.

>Jesus really hates hypocrites. There's no other word for it. They go around telling everyone that they have the answers to all their questions, even though they're just as screwed up as the rest of us. That's how people see Christians, which means we have to work hard at taking the stuff out of our own eyes before we even think of mentioning what's in other people's. We have to admit that we are hypocrites, because we stand for a set of values that we can't ever live up to, but that's not the same as judging others.

Re-engage

Jesus is not only saying that we shouldn't condemn people, but that we should praise and encourage too. We'll be judged and blessed in the same measure that we judge and bless.

>It would be good if we could learn to love the brothers and sisters that Jesus has given us. After years of being involved in church life, I still don't have any practical advice – only that you take the names of the people who annoy you and put them on the wall next to your bed. Pray God's blessing upon them without condition, and keep at it. Hopefully you will catch a bit of his love.

>If you go to parties or other places where people make you upset or angry, remember Jesus among the sinners, and stay a few minutes longer than you want to. Do something that shows God's love – say a kind word or pray – and in that act of loving beyond your own self-interest you will be the presence of Jesus where you are.

Airlock: Becoming

Themes: Prayer, The Law

Shark-infested waters

Decompress

Read through the passage a few times. First Jesus tells us that our honest searching will be rewarded. Then he says that we can trust him to give us the answer that we need. And then comes the answer: here's the meaning of life!

NOW READ MATTHEW 7:7–12

Immerse

Imagine that you are floating at sea in shark-infested waters. You're standing on a large, flat piece of wood which is keeping you from being eaten, but isn't exactly stable. The best place to keep your balance is in the middle – the further away from the centre you get, the more likely you are to fall off and become shark food.

>When I talk to Christians about the idea of 'God's Law', especially the bits to do with sex, I'm reminded of this picture. People seem to want to find the most extreme boundaries of his law, like some mad survivor tiptoeing around the edge of his raft. They don't ask, 'Where is the centre of God's will, the safest place?' They just want to know the exact point at which they will fall. And many, many people fall.

>The whole of the Sermon on the Mount is about being at the centre of God's will. Jesus basically says don't do something just because you're afraid of God's law. Do it because you love God. And then we get to the absolute centre. Jesus tells us what the whole Old Testament is about... and it's not really that complicated after all.

Re-engage

Before he gives us his reworking of the golden rule, Jesus reminds us that God is a loving, perfect father. That is the context in which we should understand his follow-on call for a radical lifestyle. Jesus wants us to be reminded of God's love and not his judgement. We should obey out of love and gratitude, not out of fear.

>Think about the one thing that you would most like someone to do for you, and do it for someone else. It's good to understand each other and learn what those things are – the things that communicate love and value, the things that bind friendships, the things that are just fun. When you get it right it can make a big difference. I remember very early on in my life at university, someone saying to me, 'When you're alone in your room and feeling a bit lonely, think about all the other people feeling the same way and go and visit one of them.'

Airlock: Becoming

Signs

Theme: Cost of discipleship

Decompress

Before we get into the details, let's meditate on another scripture passage that might help us understand it. '(God) wants all people to be saved and to know the truth' (1 Timothy 2:4). Just think about this verse and reflect on the God you know. Does this sound like him? Or do we carry an image of God as a cosmic bouncer who doesn't really want to let anyone into the party?

NOW READ MATTHEW 7:13,14

Immerse

Some people are 'glass half-empty' people and some are 'glass half-full' people. Which are you? I tend to see the negative, which makes me a glass half-empty, which makes me cross with Jesus at this point. Why can't more people be saved, Jesus? Maybe there's another way of reading this, given the verse we read above. It just *is* hard, not because God makes it that way but because of who we are. We should be glad that some of us find the way.

>But if I take one wrong step, am I going to miss the road forever? This is one of the problems of over-analysing a Bible passage all on it's own. Immediately before these words are spoken, Jesus talks about serving others, and then afterwards he starts talking about false prophets. What do these ideas have in common? Well, the connection with the next bit is obvious (it's an introduction), but there is definitely a connection with the stuff before.

>Jesus is saying, yes it's hard to find the door, but here I am, the door, right before you. Listen to what I have to say, because it's like an invaluable map on your journey.

Re-engage

Some people see being a Christian as a place you arrive at, a gate you go through. Others see it as a journey. Jesus says it's both, and we need to keep both in mind. He's the way into this whole project, because we have given our life to him, but that's just the beginning – now we have to follow him!

>Recall the time you made a decision to follow Jesus or became aware that you were already his. What were the key things that helped you make that decision? Think about talking to someone about this stuff, about God's good news in your life. Now spend some time in quiet, asking God if there is any particular step he wants you to take next in your life.

Airlock: Becoming

Many Christians think of guidance as a long-term thing. They want to know what God has got in store for them in years to come. Yet every journey, however long, is really a succession of micro-journeys, and all we have to do is take the right road each day to get to our destination. Always looking for our final stop will make us miss the beauty on the way, and we're more likely to trip over the boulders that are strewn across our path…

Extra_1 Psalm 43
Extra_2 Mark 12:30

Themes: Injustice, Trust, Anger

It's not fair!

Decompress

'Lord, when my life feels unfair, help me know that you're always with me, and that you can always be trusted.'

NOW READ PSALM 11

Immerse

Everyone else is having an easy time while we suffer. Does that sound familiar? Sometimes it can be hard to stay true to God when we're going through tough times. It often feels like life would be much simpler if we forgot about God and followed our own desires. It's even worse when the people who are making us feel bad seem to be having a much easier time of it than we are. What's the point of struggling to live a life for God, and suffering, while our friends who don't give God a second thought have an easy life?

>But sometimes we need to take a step back from our own problems, and try to see the bigger picture. When someone is making life difficult, our natural instinct is to defend ourselves. But do we ever stop to think why that person is giving us a hard time? Perhaps they are actually hurting more than we are, or perhaps they want the best for us.

>God loves us and will always be on our side; all we need to do is trust in his eternal plan for our lives. But do your 'enemies' have that sort of security?

Re-engage

While others question the fairness of God, the psalmist responds with absolute confidence in God's power and justice. When life for you, or those you love, feels totally unfair, do you still have this much confidence in God? Or do you get angry and defensive?

>Are there any situations in your life at the moment that make you want to yell at God, 'It's not fair!' Try writing down your thoughts in a journal or email to yourself – however angry or bitter it sounds! Then take a few minutes, or days, to pray about the situation. Ask God to help you understand the bigger picture. Then look again at what you've written, and hand the whole situation over to God. Delete or tear up your angry thoughts and read Psalm 11 again as a statement of your renewed trust in God.

Airlock: Becoming

Themes: Lying, Injustice, Trust

Painful honesty

Decompress

Think about the conversations you've overheard in the last 24 hours – on the bus, in the classroom or office, on a TV chat show or news broadcast, in an Internet chat room. How many lies do you think you heard? How many lies have you told?

NOW READ PSALM 12

Immerse

Have you ever played Cheat – the card game in which you have to cheat to win? I'm terrible at it, because I'm not very good at bluffing. But often it can be quite revealing, when friends you'd always thought to be honest end up being the best liars and win the game.

>Of course, in a different situation, lying comes very easily to me:

'Yes, I love your new trousers, they really flatter your figure.'

'Sorry, I can't afford to give any money to your charity appeal.'

'No, of course I wasn't talking about you behind your back, it was…'

>Lying is often regarded as a necessary evil in society, be it an innocent white lie told to spare a friend's feelings or the excuses we give to avoid trouble. Lying is part of life, and we all do it. But God calls us to be pure and truthful – like him. Quite a challenge! No wonder the psalmist says that there are no true believers left on earth.

>Staying true to God means always telling the truth – even if it will make life more difficult for us. But like the psalmist, when we feel alone and are afraid to speak the truth, we can ask God for his help and protection.

Re-engage

Have you ever found out that someone lied to you? How did you feel? Even if our original motive for lying is good, lies have a tendency to escalate and usually end up causing pain in the long run. But sometimes telling the truth can alienate us from our friends, who might call us traitors or cowards, or just pathetic. Should we tell the truth always?

>If someone has lied to you, it can be very hard to trust them again. Are you someone that people feel they can trust? Make a conscious effort not to tell any lies for the next 24 hours. If this is too easy, try doing it for a week, and so on.

Airlock: Becoming

Hello?

Themes: Depression, Trust

Decompress

'Prayer is like a telephone for us to talk to Jesus', or so goes the familiar children's chorus. But sometimes it feels like he's ignoring our calls. Have you had trouble getting through to God lately?

NOW READ PSALM 13

Immerse

Our emotions can have a big effect on the level of our faith in God. When we're at a big Christian event like Soul Survivor or Spring Harvest, we can see God at work all around us and it feels easy to trust God. But when we get home, and go back to school, university or work, it suddenly gets harder. Problems hit us, we get into arguments with our parents, we get ill, we get dumped by our girlfriend or boyfriend. And sometimes we wonder where God is in all our mess? Has he forgotten about us?

>The Psalms are so great because they contain raw emotion. The writers never try to hide any of their emotions from God – anger, despair, bitterness, hopelessness – because they knew that nothing could be hidden from God. He knows exactly how we're feeling, and he wants us to be completely honest with him. God doesn't expect us to be happy and cheerful all the time. He understands the difficulties of life, and knows that often we feel depressed, and find it hard to pray at all, let alone sing heartfelt praises.

>But this psalm ends on a puzzling note of joy. Puzzling because it seems completely at odds with the rest of the psalm. How does the writer move from complete despair to joyful praise so quickly? He does it by calling out to God from his place of pain, and trusting that God loves him and will help him, as he has done in the past. The psalmist's painful circumstances and feelings may not have changed, but his attitude towards God has, allowing him to accept the present and look forward to the future with joy.

Re-engage

The psalm can be divided into three sections – pain, prayer and praise. When you don't feel like you can joyfully praise God, try using this as a framework for your own prayer. Tell him, truthfully, exactly how you feel; ask him to help you; and thank him for the times he's helped you in the past.

Airlock: Becoming

Themes: Foolishness, Wisdom

You're a fool!

Decompress

'Lord, the world is full of fools, and I'm one of them. Help me to know more of your wisdom so that I can reveal more of your love to those around me.'

NOW READ PSALM 14

Immerse

I love the part in *Fellowship of the Ring* where Gandalf and Saruman have their big wizard's fight and then Gandalf escapes on the back of a huge eagle.

>Saruman has joined forces with the evil Sauron because he believes it is the only way to save himself, whereas Gandalf still believes in the power of goodness to defeat evil. From a worldly perspective, it's easy to see that Saruman has chosen the easier and more logical path; he can't beat Sauron so he has joined him instead. He believes Gandalf to be a fool because he has chosen the path that will logically only lead to death. However, we can see that Saruman is the foolish one, not because he was stupid or weak, but because he had turned his back on goodness.

>This is the sort of fool that Psalm 14 is talking about – people who deliberately turn their back on God. But, to a greater or lesser extent, we are all fools. We all turn our back on God at times, and do things we know he wouldn't want us to do. When reading this psalm, it's important not to get too self-righteous and judgemental of others; instead we must remember to constantly ask the Lord for his help so that we remain among those who do what is right and share in God's ultimate victory.

Re-engage

It is easy to read this psalm and to start thinking about other people – those who give us a hard time because we're Christians are all fools, but we're wise because we believe in God and know the truth. But the emphasis in this psalm is on what we do rather than what we believe. When the Lord looks down from heaven, he cannot find anyone who is doing good, even among the believers. No one is turning to God for help, no one is helping the poor. Although we are not saved by our good deeds, if we are filled with God's love, this should be evident in the way we live our lives.

If someone was to turn a spotlight on your life, how much of what was revealed would reflect God's love? How much of it would make you feel foolish in God's sight?

Airlock: Becoming

Themes: Worship, Forgiveness

We're not worthy!

Decompress

Imagine that you're about to meet someone who knows you better than anyone else. It's someone you love, who's crazy about you. But it's someone you've hurt, lied to, betrayed. You don't deserve to be forgiven but you know you will be.

>How will you prepare for this meeting?

NOW READ PSALM 15

Immerse

I used to go out with my mates every Saturday night. We'd stagger back home and finally fall into bed around 4 am. Then we'd drag ourselves out of bed five hours later, pour coffee down our throats and walk to church – often in the clothes we'd been in the night before. We'd arrive late, find some seats at the back and then force our eyes to stay open for the worship, knowing that we could easily get half an hour's sleep during the sermon! We felt quite proud of ourselves for our devotion. But being tired and hungover wasn't the best way to enter the presence of God.

>This psalm is all about how we should live our lives as followers of God. It lists the characteristics of those who may enter God's presence. The good news is that it's not a list of conditions we have to fulfil in order to enter God's presence, but descriptions of the people who are already living their lives for God. We may fail to live up to these, but if we admit our failings and ask for forgiveness, God can begin changing us into people like those described. We can enter into God's presence with confidence, knowing that once we belong to him, he won't let us be destroyed.

Re-engage

Although we are all free to enter into God's presence without fear, thanks to Jesus' death on the cross we shouldn't take this privilege for granted. When we come before God in prayer or worship, it is a good idea to first take some time to think about anything we have thought, done or said that might damage our relationship with him. This is not so that we can wallow in our failure, but so that we remember that God loves us enough to forgive anything we have done; he longs to be close to us and to walk alongside us all the time.

>If you're going to church this Sunday, try getting up a little bit earlier than usual and spend some time preparing yourself to enter into God's presence.

Airlock: Becoming

'The wicked upset the plans of the poor, but the Lord will protect them' (Psalm 14:6).

The Lord works through us. Find out about a charity or organisation that helps the poor and needy, and see if there is a way you could help. There might be a local homeless shelter where you could volunteer; or perhaps you could organise a sponsored event at your church to raise money for an aid agency who work with refugees.

Check out these websites to get some ideas:

www.christianaid.org.uk
www.oxfam.com
www.worldvision.org.uk
www.tearfund.org

Extra_1 Proverbs 22:22,23
Extra_2 James 2:1–13

| Themes: | Rights, Grace, Litigation |

Know your rights

Decompress

Who do you hate? Who really annoys you? Has anyone done something to you that is unfair?

>'Father in heaven, you are holy. May your kingdom come and your will be done in my life as well as in heaven. You supply all my needs. Please forgive me for the things I have done that have wronged you... as I forgive those who have wronged me.'

NOW READ 1 CORINTHIANS 6:1-11

Immerse

It is probably a good thing for the Christians in Corinth that this was a letter rather than a personal visit from Paul! Paul can hardly contain his anger at the way they are behaving. They were asserting their rights over each other, instead of considering their responsibilities towards each other as fellow believers.

>Instead of going to court and suing each other, their lives should have been characterised by grace and forgiveness.

>Instead of arguing publicly, they should have been living in such a way that their lives were a public statement about Jesus.

>They were trying to assert their rights over each other, rather than being prepared to allow the other to 'win'. But if both parties had been prepared to seek the best for the other, then the Christian community would have been unique in a world of litigation, feud and arguments.

>Being a Christian is not about enforcing our rights, but about acting with grace towards one another.

Re-engage

We probably don't resort to legal action, but how often do we state our rights? 'I am allowed to...' 'You can't do that to me...' 'That's not fair...' Is 'an eye for an eye, and a tooth for a tooth' a description of how we live?

>Jesus' response was: 'I tell you ... if someone slaps you on the right cheek, turn to him the other cheek as well. If someone wants to sue you in court and take your shirt, let him have your coat as well ...' (Matthew 5:39,40)

>Reread verse 11. Think about the people you don't get on with. What would your relationship be like if you tried to do what is best for them, rather than what is best for you? If you are prepared to try, God's Spirit will help you.

Airlock: Becoming

Themes: Honouring God, Sex

Sex in the city

Decompress
Write a list of the important things in your life. Number them in order of priority, with the most important one first. Ask God to help you have the same priorities that he has. Ask him to help you to see things his way.

NOW READ 1 CORINTHIANS 6:1–20

Immerse
I can visit places on the other side of the world without leaving my chair. I can communicate with people who share the same interests as me. The Internet has opened up loads of possibilities. But not all parts of the Internet are safe. It is a place where con men will try to rip you off, where people will pretend to be something they are not to exploit you, and where there are all manner of disgusting images.

>Possibilities bring choices. Just because we can do something, it doesn't mean that we should. This principle can be applied to anything from genetic engineering to sexual ethics.

>God has something to say to his creation and to those who he put in charge of it. Ultimately, the universe exists for his enjoyment and glory, not so that we can exploit it.

Re-engage
'How far can I go?' That's the question I wanted answered when I was a teenager – how much was permissible without technically breaking God's standards. It's an important question to have answered so that we can set boundaries. But it's not the most important question.

>'What is honouring to God?' is the most important question (verse 20). In practical terms the answer will probably be less permissive than the technical answer to the first question, but it's an important one to think through before you get into a relationship, when you begin a relationship, and as the relationship continues. It's a matter of priority – sexual gratification or God-pleasing?

>The same question is important in every area of our lives. The Corinthians had problems with their sexual morals, and we may have similar problems. But the principle can be applied to any area of our lives – what is most important: God's pleasure and glory or our pleasure? Think about the way we use money, the things we buy and our attitude to them, the things we watch or listen to...

>Look again at the list you made earlier and ask that question about those things.

Airlock: Becoming

Agony uncle

Themes: Relationships, Sex, Advice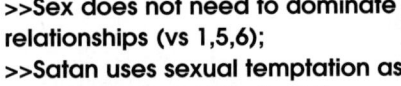

Decompress

Imagine that you could write a letter to God and get answers to all the questions. What would you ask him? Why do you want to know those things? The amazing thing is that we don't even have to write – we can speak with him directly, and he has written the answers to our questions even before we asked him. That is one of the things that makes the Bible such an incredible book.

NOW READ 1 CORINTHIANS 7:1–7

Immerse

If you look in almost any magazine, there will be people offering advice – about legal or financial matters, about health problems or sexual techniques, about relationships of one form or another. Think of this part of 1 Corinthians as an agony uncle's reply...

>Human behaviour has been reduced to a combination of genetic programming and evolutionary instincts. The common phrase for this is 'it's only natural'. Paul challenged that approach to human sexual behaviour in these verses:
>>Monogamy (one sexual partner for life) is natural (v 2);
>>Marriage partners have mutual responsibilities (vs 3,4);
>>Sex does not need to dominate relationships (vs 1,5,6);
>>Satan uses sexual temptation as a weapon against us (vs 2,5).

>The first three aspects of sex need to be stated because of the reality of the fourth. In our contemporary society, we are bombarded by more images and messages about sex than in Corinth. We need to be aware of all four principles in order that we live in a way that honours God.

Re-engage

Sit down and divide a sheet of paper into four columns with the following headings: more than one partner for life; exploiting partners; sex dominates; sexual temptation.

>While you are watching TV ask yourself which of the four principles are demonstrated or flaunted by what you watch and write it down in the appropriate column. At the end of the evening look at everything you have written.

>This is probably a typical evening. Becoming aware of it is the first step in combatting Satan's deception and lies. Ask God to help you to see through the lies and to live the truth. You might want to make a 'True Love Waits' style pledge to God (check out www.truelovewaits.com).

Airlock: Becoming

Themes: Singleness, Marriage

For better or for worse?

Decompress
Think about all the people who are significant in your life. Thank God for the different relationships you have with others – family, friends, boyfriend or girlfriend, colleagues, teachers, counsellors...

NOW READ 1 CORINTHIANS 7:8–16

Immerse
Human beings are created for relationships and struggle in isolation. Primarily we are created to have a relationship with God, but we are also born to relate to each other in many different ways.

>Paul gives a number of rulings and answers. We should remember that they are answers to specific questions sent in a previous letter, so we need to be careful about applying them to our context without asking first of all whether they were intended to be universal principles or localised answers (see verse 17 for a universal principle).

>In all of these different relationships, Paul wants the Corinthians to want do what God wants, not to give in to pressures from their society. Remember that these words were written to Christians struggling to live in a way that honoured God within a sex-mad society.

>In all relationships, we should bear in mind the principles behind Paul's advice here: relationships are important and we should work hard at making them work. With non-believers we should bear in mind (and pray for) the possibility of conversion. We also need to bear in mind whether the relationship honours God, and if not, how it can.

Re-engage
What about going out with non-Christians? Doesn't this passage suggest that it's okay because we can bring them to Christ? The implication of these words is the Christian was in the relationship before they came to faith. In this context, Paul is saying that the believer should work at the relationship for the sake of the family, the possibility of conversion and the importance of marriage. So this passage doesn't endorse going out with non-Christians, but it doesn't prohibit it either. If you have doubts, perhaps it would be better not to start a relationship that is going to fall short of God's standards.

>Review any relationships that you are in at the moment, or may be thinking of embarking on.

Airlock: Becoming

Themes: Ambition, Calling

Be the best

Decompress

What are your ambitions? What do you dream of being or doing? If you could do anything at all with your life, what would it be? What is your life like now? Is it as exciting or glamorous as your dreams and ambitions? Do you want to be who God created you to be?

NOW READ 1 CORINTHIANS 7:17–24

Immerse

A new Christian was talking to her non-Christian friends and said, 'People say I have changed, but I haven't, I'm still the same me.' She lived in the same house and had the same friends but her friends had noticed the difference God had made in her life.

>Jesus called his first disciples to leave their lifestyle behind and follow him. He calls us to follow him too. But Paul wanted the Corinthians to know that living a radical lifestyle does not necessarily mean making radical changes. Those who were slaves did not have to campaign for their freedom. 'Each of you should stay as you were when you were called, and stay there with God' (verse 24).

>We are called to serve Jesus where we are until he calls us elsewhere. The last two words of verse 24 are the key – 'with God.'

Being with God is the best we can get. It beats money, status, power or any other measure of success that we might choose because it has an eternal dimension. If we are with God, we will always be with God. But we won't always have money, status or power.

>Our ambition should be to be with God. He wants us to live our lives with him. We can achieve that where we are, although there may be times when he wants us to be with him somewhere else and we have to change our circumstances.

Re-engage

Write a list of your ambitions – be honest and realistic, but don't be afraid to be ambitious. Now look at the list of values in Galatians 5:22,23. These are the qualities of someone who spends their time with God.

>If it is possible to achieve your ambitions without compromising any of those qualities, then pursue it for all you are worth. God will make it clear to you if he has other plans for you.

>If pursuing your ambitions will compromise one or more of those qualities, then you would be wise to think carefully and ask God to show you the way ahead.

Airlock: Becoming

In the High Court today
a Writ was issued
by God.

He was claiming unspecified damages
for emotional distress
caused by Breach of Promise.

In the Particulars of Claim, millions of
broken promises were listed: all starting,
"God, if you will just help me…"

It was a class action
which was dismissed because
there were too many defendants.

© Nick Lear 2002

Extra_1 **Luke 11:1–13**
Extra_2 **Ephesians 6:18**

Theme: Commitment to God

Do you need reheating?

Decompress
'Lord, please help me understand what it means to be on fire for you.'

NOW READ HOSEA 6:1 – 7:2

Immerse
Have you ever been really keen on something for a few weeks, then for no real reason just given up on it? It could have been a sport or a musical instrument. Or perhaps you started a book, read the first few chapters and then never got round to finishing it. It's something I do all the time – I've got a pile of books by the side of my bed which I'm trying to find the time (and energy) to finish.

>This passage explains how God wants people to really get to know him and stay with him. 'I want faithful love' and 'I want people to know me' (v 6) really show what God is saying here. If our love for God has gone a bit cold, he wants us to reheat it so that we can constantly be with him!

>Hosea was a prophet who was trying his hardest to get the nations to remember that, even though they were experiencing a time of prosperity, God still wanted to be amongst them.

Re-engage
Verse 6 shows us what God really wants of us: 'I want faithful love more than I want animal sacrifices. I want people to know me more than I want burnt offerings.' Would he prefer us to put hundreds of pounds into the collection at church once a week, or to get to know him by spending time with him every day?

>TV often takes over my life. There's generally at least one programme that I have to watch every week, and I end up getting ruled by it. Maybe you are 'ruled' by something else. For just one day a week, try not doing this activity that you're ruled by – instead, find a quiet place and spend time with God, talking to him and giving him room to speak to you. Maybe take your Bible and copy of *Airlock* and spend this time reading them. It could be what you need to really get to know God – he's a friend who is worth getting to know better!

Airlock: Becoming

| Theme: | Putting God first |

If you can't stand the heat

Decompress
'Lord, thanks for always being with me, even when I forget you are! Please help me understand what this passage means to the way I live my life.'

NOW READ HOSEA 7:3–7

Immerse
Microwave cookers are today's wonder utility. They are in our house anyway! Unless our meal is cooked in just one big pot, we can never get the timings right and everything ends up being ready at different times, so something usually ends up in the microwave being reheated.

>But microwaves can also be quite dangerous. I heard that one man used to watch his food being cooked in the microwave. Unfortunately his microwave was faulty and the 'micro waves' that do the cooking were actually coming out from the cooker and slowly cooking him – he was slowly cooked from the inside out. I also heard another story where an elderly lady used to dry her pet poodle in the oven, on low heat of course, after it had been bathed. When she bought a microwave she thought she could do the same thing. What she didn't know was that microwaves cook from the inside out, unlike her old electric cooker – if you've seen *Gremlins* then you know what happened!

>Ovens, whether ancient, modern or even microwaves, cook and burn. The people in this passage are likened to ovens because they are burning up their rulers. The country is falling apart because they don't talk to God.

Re-engage
God wants us to put him first in everything we do. It is not simply about putting God first at church or in our small groups of Christian friends, but when we are with our friends/at work/with our family. It's about putting God first in all our choices. It's about putting God first wherever we are, and whatever we're doing.

>Look for a situation that you can defuse. Turn to God and ask him what you should do instead of adding to the fire.

Airlock: Becoming

Themes: Making decisions, God

Burnt pizza

Decompress
'God, please guide me through these words so that I can understand what you want me to know.'

NOW READ HOSEA 7:8–16

Immerse
Cooking a pizza can be quite difficult. I know, all you have to do is stick it in the oven, but my old oven used to either burn the base to a cinder or leave the top completely frozen so that you had to finish off the job in the microwave. Have you ever eaten burnt pizza? Yeuch! The good taste has gone, plus it won't give you much energy either because you've burnt it away!

>Verse 9 speaks about this – the people don't go back to God for help when they're in trouble, which causes them to burn away. Instead they put their hope in two foreign nations, and this makes them lose their flavour.

>In verse 14, Hosea talks about people lying on their beds crying, asking for grain and new wine. Which is just like saying 'sorry' for doing something wrong, but then continuing to do it and expecting that you'll be given a present in return. It doesn't work like that!

Re-engage
Friends are a massive influence on our lives. They can shape the kinds of music we listen to, the way we spend our spare time, the opinions we have about important issues, the decisions we make on a day-to-day basis. They can even lead us astray.

>Think about your friends. Are they a good or a bad influence on your life? What does God want us to consider in our choice of friends? Do they have to be Christians? Thank God for all your friends, asking him to help you be a good witness.

>Spend time asking God to be part of your decision-making. You might find it helpful to make a list of all the decisions you've got to make in the next week or so, and then to go through the list praying about each one of them. Keep a note in your prayer journal, so that you can look back in the coming weeks and months and see where God has led you. You never know, God may lead you into places that you never thought you'd reach!

Airlock: Becoming

Themes:	Worship, Idols

'I told you so...'

Decompress
'Lord, please help me put aside all that I've got to do today/that has gone on today and concentrate on what you are saying to me through this passage.'

NOW READ HOSEA 8:1–10

Immerse
Have you ever asked for advice from a friend, and then decided to ignore it? I have, and when doing things my own way went wrong, I had to suffer the consequences! The worse bit was admitting that I'd ignored my friends' advice and hearing the chorus of 'I told you so!' which seemed to echo around the room.

>It is not always appropriate to do exactly what your friends tell you to do. But God's advice is different. He always knows what is best for us. After all, he can even foresee our futures. This passage shows us how upset God becomes when we ignore him. He hates it when we forget him and put other things first in our lives, as he knows what this can lead to.

Re-engage
It's really easy to make events, objects and even people more important than God in our lives. Consider what you can do to help put God back at the top of your priority list.

>Why not organise an event or activity for your friends that combines your favourite pastimes with the purpose of glorifying God. It could be anything from a PlayStation evening, where you first study something in the Bible (eg what it means to 'run the race') before you actually play on the PlayStation. Or you could watch your favourite TV programme, and then discuss which characters showed how God would, or would not, want us to act. You could also do an activity based on helping others, eg giving time regularly to visit or help a lonely person on your street.

>What things in your life can easily become idols? How can you reduce their influence? How can you use these things for God's purpose?

Airlock: Becoming

Themes: Giving, Trusting in God

Giving for the sake of it

Decompress

'Jesus, thank you for always being with me. Please help me to understand what you want me to learn through this passage. Thank you.'

NOW READ HOSEA 8:11–14

Immerse

If you have played the game Jenga you'll know that a strong tower can soon become a weak one when only a couple of bricks are taken away. Eventually, if we're not very careful, the whole thing comes crashing to the ground. It's like that with our lives too! If we do not have strong back-up around us, life can easily fall apart when things go wrong.

>The people in Israel built more places to worship in and sacrificed more animals but forgot the most important part, actually spending time with God and trusting in him. It's as if they were buying gifts but forgetting what the actual purpose of giving is.

>The last two lines of verse 14 are given as a warning to the people to trust in God, something that they'd obviously not been doing!

Re-engage

Think about the times when you give a gift – at Christmas, or for someone's birthday; do you give gifts because you have to, or as God would give? Think about some different ways of giving that would show people God's love for them. Think about someone you know who is going through a difficult patch. Buy or make them something to cheer them up. Why not wrap it up nicely and write a Bible verse on the gift tag?

>How do you worship God? Is your 'quiet time' with God always the same, a ritual? Does the place, time and way of doing the 'quiet time' stop you really meeting with God? Do it differently today and really meet with God.

>For instance, if you usually have a quiet time just before going to bed, why not bring it forward to the daytime and get out into the fresh air – find a field or a local beauty spot and spend some time reading your Bible and praying as part of God's creation.

Airlock: Becoming

How can you become more committed to God? What things do you need to change to help you do this? What things get in your way?

Exodus 20:4-6
Mark 1:1-20

Themes: Healing, Getting attention

Walking and leaping

Decompress

Quick recap:
'Peter and John went to pray
They met a lame man on the way
He asked for alms and held out his palms
And this is what Peter did say
Silver and gold have I none
But what I do have I give thee
In the name of Jesus Christ
Of Nazareth, get up and walk.'
(*Anon.*)

NOW READ ACTS 3:11–26

Immerse

Every so often, the electrical shop down the road pays some poor guy to stand outside the shop with a microphone and an amp and rave loudly about the lovely deals they've got inside. 'Roll up, roll up,' he'll shout into the microphone without any warning, startling a passing old lady and causing her to drop her shopping. 'Come inside and check out our fantastic prices.'

>The trouble with this approach, which the shop hasn't realised yet, is that blocking the doorway and startling passers-by won't entice them into the shop. They're doing something with the aim of drawing a crowd, and end up driving people away. It's just not that easy attracting people's attention. Unless, that is, your name is Peter.

>Peter must have known when he healed the lame man that it was going to cause a bit of a fuss. And sure enough it attracted a crowd. 'What happened?' 'Didn't he used to be lame?' 'How come he's walking and leaping and praising God?' etc.

>So Peter was ready for the questions that came his way, and being the man of the moment, he seized the opportunity to preach, redirecting the crowd's attention from the lame man, himself and John, on to God. He gave a great little summary of everything that had happened in the last few years, linking the recent history of Jesus' life and resurrection in with events as far back as Abraham and Moses. Now that's what I call a gifted preacher.

Re-engage

The guy who was healed was a beggar on the street. How do you react when faced with someone begging? Do you walk past and feel guilty for not giving them money? Or do you give them all the loose change in your pocket? How about following the example of Peter and praying for them. I'm not suggesting that you make a big fuss – but pray silently, asking God to be with that person.

Airlock: Becoming

Themes: Trials, Persecution, Faith

Arrested development

Decompress
'Lord, give me the courage to be loyal to you, even when things aren't going the way I want.'

NOW READ ACTS 4:1–4

Immerse
I've never been to prison. I've no real intention of going either. I did go to boarding school for five years, and at times that was like a prison – bars on the dormitory windows, slop at meal times, lights out after 10 pm. But it wasn't prison.

>This passage got me thinking. Would I ever end up in prison because of my faith? Would I ever get taken away by the authorities for evangelising? OK, I don't live in a country where being a Christian is illegal, but still? Would I be willing to put my future on the line in order to tell people the good news about Jesus? Would you?

>So when Peter and John end up being carted off to prison and an uncertain future, it looks like they've failed. But Luke gives us a fantastic closing statistic – OK, Peter and John have been arrested, but many of those who heard Peter preach believed, so that there were five thousand Christians (and that's only counting the men)!

>If we go back just three short chapters to the beginning of the book of Acts, we find a group of disciples who are waiting for stuff to happen, meeting in secret. In just a short period of time, the boldness of the disciples and the truth of the message of Jesus has seen a huge increase in conversions. Exciting times indeed. But also lingering on the horizon, is the threat of something nasty... The early church is going through a period of amazing growth, but it'll soon be going through a period of shocking persecution as well.

>Our walk with Jesus is always about more than what we can immediately see.

Re-engage
Hard as it is to believe, in our safe, cosy, biscuit-infested world of Christianity, but people are still put in jail or killed for their faith. Read more about what goes on in other countries online at www.csw.org.uk and www.opendoors.org. Find out what you can do to help those who are incarcerated for their faith, like writing letters to heads of state, and your MP, and then do it!

Airlock: Becoming

Themes: Justice, Proof

Twelve angry men

Decompress
'Lord, when difficult trials and tests come my way, give me the strength to stand up like Peter and John, without despair, knowing that your plans will be carried out.'

NOW READ ACTS 4:5–22

Immerse
Ever been told off by someone when you've done nothing wrong? Or blamed for something that wasn't your fault? I remember being sent out of a maths test for cheating, when it was my neighbour who had been leaning over, talking to me and trying to see what I'd written. I felt angry for being accused of something I didn't do. I felt betrayed by my friend who'd cheated and got me sent out. And I was upset that the teacher hadn't believed my innocence.

>Peter and John had far more at stake than failing a maths test, though… They were up in court for doing something wrong, when in fact they'd done something right. They'd healed a man by the authority of Jesus. The Jewish leaders weren't particularly thrilled by this, especially as the evidence was right there in front of them – a middle-aged man jumping up and down and flexing his leg muscles. So, after plenty of deliberation, they came to the conclusion that they'd have to let these uneducated miracle-performing fishermen go.

Re-engage
It must have been hard for these highly educated Jewish leaders to understand how two such fishermen could speak so eloquently, and how they had the power to heal someone. It must have been even harder for them to hear the name of Jesus, especially as they thought they'd stamped out that particular 'cult' at the crucifixion.

>It just goes to show, though, that God can use anyone to spread the gospel, and that his power can't be stopped by human means.

>Peter and John were very eloquent in their defence, so much so that they shocked the Jewish leaders. How eloquent are you when someone asks you why you're a Christian? Why not try writing down in advance what you believe and why – that way, when difficult conversations crop up, you'll be prepared.

Airlock: Becoming

| Themes: | Courage, Fear |

Dutch courage

Decompress
Ever been scared? Really, really scared? What did you do?

NOW READ ACTS 4:23-31

Immerse
Things that I'm afraid of:
>>Public speaking.
>>Heights.
>>Public speaking in a high place.
>>Ridicule.
>>Public nudity (this tends to go hand in hand with ridicule).
>>Public speaking in a high place while naked. (That's what is commonly known as labouring the point!)
>>Nasty things happening to my loved ones.
>>Sharks.
>>Ravioli.
>>Dentists.
>>The threat of persecution.

>This may have been the moment when the believers first got the idea that spreading the good news about Jesus wasn't going to be an easy task, and that the big black cloud which was coming their way was persecution.

>Their response? Straight away, they prayed. 'Dear Lord, we know that people are making nasty threats, but help us not to be scared.' And God answered their prayer – 'They spoke God's word without fear.'

>The same can happen for us. Scared? Then pray...

Re-engage
What are you afraid of at the moment? Failing exams? Not getting into the university of your choice? Failing in a relationship? Being scared is a horrible feeling because of the sense of helplessness that goes along with it – but we *can* do something about any fears that we may have. We can take them to God, and know that he will help us to deal with them.

>Write a list in your prayer journal of the things you are afraid of, and pray about them, asking God to help ease your fears. Check back in the coming weeks and months to see how God has answered your prayers.

>If you need further reassurance, try reading Psalm 27. It's a great reminder that when we follow Jesus and trust in him, he can help us let go of our fears.

Airlock: Becoming

Themes: Unity, Sharing

One for all, all for one

Decompress
Socialism tends to get a bit of a bad press these days. Prepare to read about socialism done the right way – the Jesus way.

NOW READ ACTS 4:32–37

Immerse
OK, confession time – I can get obsessed with buying 'stuff'. I must have the latest CDs by all my favourite artists. And the latest DVDs with my favourite actors in. And the latest books by all my favourite authors. And that's not to mention the latest PlayStation 2 games...

>But all the spending I do doesn't improve my life any. Sure, it may make me happy for five minutes that I've got a bargain in the HMV sale, but I've slowly and gradually reached the conclusion that my belongings don't actually make me any happier. What does improve my life is my relationships with my friends, my family, and most importantly, God. So what's worth concentrating on? The latest CD or spending time praying? I think the answer is obvious.

Re-engage
So how do I go about changing my world view from that of a consumer into something which more closely resembles what God wants? It's a tough question, but one thing I've started to do is budget. And I don't just mean money, although it's helped to cut down the amount of money I spend on irrelevant stuff like CDs – I've also tried to budget my time better as well. This makes time for the important, non-urgent things like praying and reading my Bible, at the expense of all the non-important urgent things I do, like finishing the level on my newest PlayStation game.

>What things in your life are important but not urgent? How are you going to prioritise them over the urgent, non-important stuff that seems to get in the way?

>Is there someone else you know who's having the same problems with budgeting their time and money? Could you get together every week and talk about how you've been getting on? Being accountable is a great incentive to change the way you act in difficult situations.

Airlock: Becoming

trol 84427 8727142 ...

GENTS BIKE 3speed gears hardly used tel 84427 821259 £25

NAVY/BURGUNDY stripe sofa 3 seater crowson fabric good condition £50 buyer collects 84427 859948

TOILET COMPLETE with cistern and seat/lid twyfords modern design champagne (light) colour £25ono 84427 846783

ARMCHAIR UPHOLSTERED with wooden legs high seat suits older person as new ex.con £40ono 84427 846783

DROP FRONT cabinet with cupboard under suitable as bureau or drinks cabinet ex con £50ono 84427 846783

DINING/LOUNGE unit for cutlery/crockery 4 drawers 2doors 102cmWx75cmH ex cond £75ono 84427 846783

DOUBLE GLAZED front door 80x205 aluminium frame left hand open keys as new £30 84427 221827

SONY MUSIC centre record deck tapex2 cd radio g.w.o £50 84427 240584

GAN CHICCO travel system inc footmuff suitable from birth cream check only £75 collection only 84427 964204

TABLE TENNIS table full size £35 84427 589516 84427 960735

POLYETHYLENE PREFORMED garden pool 4'x3' approx vgc £25 84427 226444

41" DIAMETER round mahogany table 4 chairs at a bargan price of £25 84427 258715

DREAMLAND OVERBLANKET (luxury harmony) 195x195cms duel controls £15 84427 342610

RUG ROUND 48" dia brown fawn cream luxurious wool made from kit new £70 84427 844279

TODDLER TRIKE with push along handle elc £10 84427 041560

TABLE LAMPS shades lights all under £25 84427 343543

ELECTROLUX upright vacuum cleaner ex working order with tools £35 4 bar stools £20 84427 843543

Have a look around at the things you own. Do you own them or do they own you? Is there anything you have that you *wouldn't* be prepared to sell? That's when you know you've got a problem. How about having a car boot sale and getting rid of a lot of your stuff.
You could give any money raised to the charity of your choice.

Also, try budgeting your time/money better. You'll be surprised at how much it helps.

Luke 16:1-15
Mark 12:41-44

Themes: Heaven, Obedience

Beware of the wolves

Decompress

'Pass exams the easy way.' 'Get rich quick.' There's a whiff coming off those two phrases and it's mainly rat. Equally smelly is the suggestion that you can just wander into the eternal life party without knowing the host. In today's passage, some people had been saying that. Jesus calls them false prophets and dangerous wolves, which was pretty rude in those days.

NOW READ MATTHEW 7:15–23

Immerse

The door to the party is blocked by a 16-stone bruiser with a scar on the cheek and an unpleasant expression. Yup. She's pretty scary. As you approach, she stubs her cigarette out on her neck and cracks her knuckles. You look more confident than you feel. 'Hello, it's a good party by the look of it. Is Dave here yet?' There's usually a Dave at these parties.

>'Dave who?'

>'You know, Dave, well-dressed. Medium height, with hair and eyes. Erm... wears glasses? Moustache? Beard? Tattoo?'

>The most repeatable of the next words you hear is 'off'.

>Jesus suggests that people will try and con their way into the party which is his kingdom. And it may be surprising for them to see some of the people who are coming in as they go out. But they don't have to gatecrash. They're invited. We all are.

Re-engage

Jesus changes in this passage from being the gatekeeper to judge (v 23). The best way into the party is to have a relationship with the party-giver. If we want to be part of the celebration we must get to know Jesus better. And that involves more than turning up to church once a week, singing a few worship songs and switching off when the sermon gets underway.

>Work on your relationship with Jesus. Spend more time with him. Involve him in your actions. Ask him what he thinks of what you're doing.

Airlock: Becoming

Themes: Obedience, Wisdom

Building regulations

Decompress

You may recall singing, 'The wise Man Built his House Upon the Rock' when you were younger (or more recently – see B/07). Can you recognise the important and life-changing message behind the words of a children's song?

>If you have some children's building bricks around somewhere, you might find it a help to fiddle with them whilst reading this. Honest!

NOW READ MATTHEW 7:24–29

Immerse

How do you know if your teacher is rubbish? Almost certainly because you are able to make a comparison with another teacher who is good. Comparisons are brilliant aids to quality control. This passage has two comparisons in it.

>Comparison 1: there are two identical houses (vs 24–27). Yet, when the storm comes along, one falls and one doesn't. So what's the difference? The foundations. Jesus tells his audience that the foundations come from listening to God's word and acting on it. Being obedient to the Bible is foundational.

>Comparison 2: there are two teaching styles (vs 28,29). The old style had seemed OK if a bit petty at times. Then along comes a new teacher and the old style is seen to be what it always was – without authority. The absence of authority had not been noticed until Jesus came along with some real authority – it made the people realise what they had been missing.

>If you are a builder, it is unbelievably embarrassing to have your own house fall down. The pile of rubble will stand as lasting testament to your inability. Not even Bob the Builder will be able to fix it.

Re-engage

You need to hear Jesus' words and act on them. Bible-reading that does not end up in action of some sort is time wasted. Our time spent with the Bible should be a life-changing experience.

>Try and make a 'to do' list which you fill in each time you read the Bible; that way you will be fruity and will also be building up your own foundations. Memo to self – building metaphor in danger of collapse.

Airlock: Becoming

Clean up your act

Themes: Healing, Law

Decompress
Pray for God to open your eyes to those who are today's outcasts – not just the beggars on our streets or the famine victims on the TV, but those nearer at hand, those victimised at school or the elderly neighbour with few visitors.

NOW READ MATTHEW 8:1-4

Immerse
When Diana, Princess of Wales, visited AIDS victims, and sat with them and held their hands, she removed a lot of the stigma about that illness. Jesus touching lepers had a similar impact.

>Jesus was followed by large crowds (v 1) and so his teaching and his every action was being scrutinised for meaning. Diana discovered that the life of a princess is never far from photographers, reporters and general mischief makers. The newspapers love a hypocrite.

>So when the leper knelt before Jesus, we can imagine the crowd standing still, keeping quiet and watching to see what he would do. Walk on by and he looks as if he lacks compassion and power; touch and heal and he breaks the Levitical law of cleanliness.

>Were the crowd the paparazzi of their day? Did they want an image of Jesus getting it wrong? Unlike today's celebrities, who frequently do get it wrong, that wasn't going to happen.

Re-engage
No illness or human condition seems to be beyond Jesus' power to heal. Know who he is and pray in faith for those who suffer.

>Healing today is a thorny subject, in that many people pray for healing from terrible illnesses, and their prayers aren't answered – they continue to suffer or even die. But some people who pray for healing do experience miracles. We can only pray in faith, and continue to trust in God that he's got everything in hand, no matter what happens.

>Why not make a point of adding one small step to your compassion for the sick and suffering? Send a card to someone who has been ill for a long time reminding them that you are still praying for them.

Airlock: Becoming

Themes: Faith, Authority, Healing

Authority figures

Decompress
Think of a time when something completely unexpected happened. What was it that turned your world on its head?

NOW READ MATTHEW 8:5–13

Immerse
This healing goes across a pretty significant cultural barrier. It isn't just between two people from different ethnic backgrounds, but between two individuals whose people are enemies. It's like the IRA healing the UDF, the Palestinian healing the Jewish settler or the black Zimbabwean healing the white farmer.

>Matthew's Gospel has turned the world on its head, yet somehow, maybe through over-exposure, the years have mellowed our shock. We need to remember that this incident occurred when a representative of an occupying army asked for compassion from one of the locals. The expected reaction would not have been warm – 'You come here, take over our land, demand we pay taxes to Caesar and now you want sympathy because your servant is ill? You know what you can do with your request for help...'

>Not only does Jesus say an instant 'yes' (v 7), though, demonstrating that his compassion knows no boundaries, but he responds to the centurion's humility by observing that he has not found such faith in the locals (v 10). So far it has been the crowds who are astonished at Jesus. Now it is Jesus' turn to be astonished.

Re-engage
Do you, by your instinct or cultural prejudice, consider some people beyond the gospel? Ask God, and perhaps some other people too, to help you see people with Jesus' eyes.

>Walk down the road and observe the people you pass – the people on their way to work, the people out shopping, those on the fringes of society, the old and infirm, the homeless. As you pass each one, make a conscious effort to see that person as Jesus would see them – with love.

>Pray for some people, or groups of people, who are seen as your traditional 'enemies'.

Airlock: Becoming

| Themes: | Prophecy, Future |

Clinical healing

Decompress
The things people do to get out of helping make the supper! Instead of helping with the food, Jesus heals the woman of the house and gets her to do it.

NOW READ MATTHEW 8:14–17

Immerse
The world today is full of attempts to predict the future. From astrology to tarot readings, palmistry to tea leaves, people are fascinated with the idea of knowing what will happen when.

>But suppose you knew? Suppose you knew that you were going to die on a particular date, or lose a leg in a car accident at a certain hour? How would you cope? Uncertainty helps us to live without undue worry.

>As Jesus awaits his future, and comes to realise his fate, he is surrounded by the accessories of godliness – healings, exorcisms and a queue of the sick and inadequate. He also knows the constant guidance of the scriptures he has grown up with, and the realisation that he is the suffering servant Isaiah talked about, who will save his people through his own death.

Re-engage
The reaction of Peter's mother-in-law after Jesus heals her is to serve him. Think about what Jesus has done for you on the cross and then think about ways in which you could serve him out of gratitude. Are there things you could volunteer to do at church? Are there any other practical ways in which you could demonstrate God's love to those around you in order to show how much he has done for you?

>Read Isaiah 52:13 – 53:12 quietly to yourself, thanking God for what he has done in Jesus. Why not write out the words of Isaiah 53:10–12, perhaps making them into a poster with the words 'Thank you' written in big letters underneath. Pin it up somewhere you'll see it regularly – perhaps by your bed. Then every time you see it, say a prayer, thanking Jesus for what he's done in your life, and for what he's going to do.

Airlock: Becoming